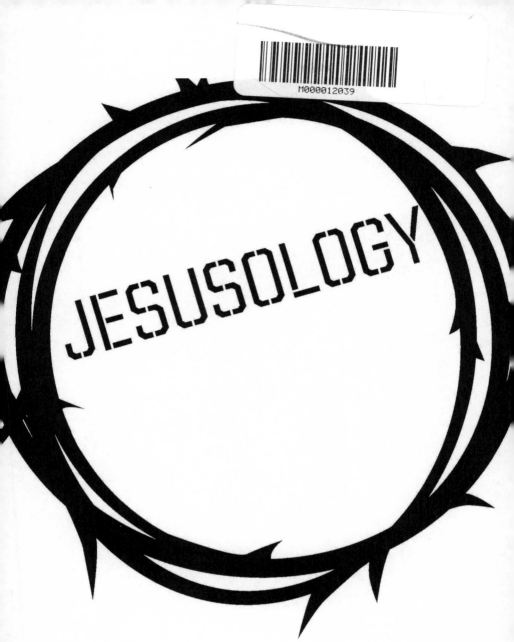

JESUSOLOGY

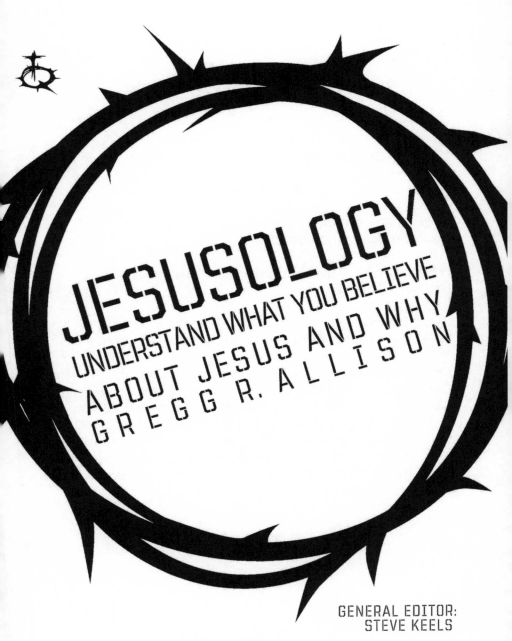

JESUSOLOGY
UNDERSTAND WHAT YOU BELIEVE
ABOUT JESUS AND WHY
GREGG R. ALLISON

GENERAL EDITOR:
STEVE KEELS

BROADMAN
& HOLMAN
PUBLISHERS

NASHVILLE, TENNESSEE

Published by Broadman & Holman Publishers,
Nashville, Tennessee

Dewey Decimal Classification: 230
Subject Heading: JESUS CHRIST \ DOCTRINAL THEOLOGY

1 2 3 4 5 6 7 8 9 10 09 08 07 06 05

CONTENTS

ABOUT

YOU: High-school student who loves God. Is serious about faith in Jesus Christ or at least interested and willing to explore Christianity. Is tired of fluff and pat answers. Is challenged by deeper discussions, including deep theology. Isn't afraid to wrestle with an issue, put it down, then have another go at it—but not with theory; it has to work and make a difference. Is certain that in the mysterious reality of human existence, a sure and true word from God is given to light and shape our experience so that we can know God and please Him.

ME: Dad to three people—one a married college graduate, another a college student, and the third a high-school student. Husband of *the best* woman. Teacher of theology. Sunday-school teacher at church. Enjoys worshipping God, working through tough issues, and hanging out with friends. Has been a pastor, missionary, church board director, college minister, soccer coach (little kids), baseball coach (Little League), and editor. Formerly from Chicago, cheers for the Cubs, the Bulls, and the Bears. Loves Jesus and students.

JESUS: The subject of this book, which discusses (1) who Jesus is as both God and man, and how His life, death, resurrection, and ascension rescued us from sin, and (2) how this salvation invades our lives and transforms everything about us from the moment we become Christians until we see Him face-to-face. Says, "I am the way, the truth, and the life. No one comes to the Father except through Me" (John 14:6), explaining that He is the *key* to enjoying a personal relationship with God.

1

THEOLOGY: The study of Jesus based on what He reveals about Himself in the entire Bible. Carefully organized by topics and clearly communicated so as to be understood and lived out concretely. Sometimes these topics are referred to as *doctrines*. A doctrine is a truth that is based on what the Bible affirms, and it impacts us in a life-changing way. We could also refer to these topics or doctrines as *beliefs*. A belief is a truth that is commonly held by Christians, not only by those who are living but also by those who have been part of the Christian church over the course of its two-thousand-year existence. Beliefs are also based on the teaching of the Bible, and they influence not only what we think but our entire lives as well. We can also call these crucial topics *truths*. A truth is a sure idea that corresponds to reality. To say that the walls of my office are painted white is a truth; to say that they are green or red is an error. The truths we will explore in this book come from the Bible. When we become convinced of them—and I urge you to develop a strong sense of certainty about them—they change our lives. Doctrines, beliefs, truths—these are the focus of theology.

THIS BOOK: Discusses you, me, Jesus, and theology. Focuses on the mystery of the incarnation of the Son of God as Jesus Christ, who was fully God and fully human. Sets forth the wonders of Christ's life of obedience, atoning death for our sins, resurrection from the dead, and ascension into heaven. Traces the work of God in applying Christ's salvation to your personal life. Highlights key passages of Scripture (in the Old and New Testaments) to understand what they say about Jesus and the salvation He offers. Shares stories about my own experience of Jesus. Offers questions and activities to encourage readers to go deeper with Jesus and experience Him in a powerful new way.

CHAPTER ONE

"BUT YOU—WHO DO YOU SAY THAT I AM?"

Ask several people who Jesus Christ is, and you may hear these answers:

- "Jesus was the founder of Christianity."
- "He was a political revolutionary who attempted to lead His Jewish compatriots in an uprising against the Roman Empire in the first century."
- "Jesus was a philosopher who taught the importance of love and nonviolence and was killed because His ideas were unpopular."
- "He was a wise teacher who went around talking about ethics and encouraging people to do good."
- "Jesus is a brand of blue jeans." (In Italy, where I lived for seven years, two hugely popular brand names are Jesus Jeans and Judas Jeans, so Italian high-school students tend to think of Jesus in terms of a clothing choice.)
- "He was a crazed maniac who mistakenly imagined He was the long-awaited Jewish messiah and died in futility attempting to persuade others of His delusion."
- "Jesus was a great prophet of Allah, though not the Son of God. And He prophesied about Muhammad, the final and greatest prophet of Allah." (This is the view of Shi'ite Muslims.)

An interesting array of ideas about Jesus Christ that, surprisingly, aren't so different from the assumptions Jesus Himself confronted during His earthly ministry nearly two thousand years ago: "When Jesus came to the region of Caesarea Philippi, He asked His disciples, 'Who do people say that the Son of Man is?' And they said, 'Some say John the Baptist; others, Elijah; still others, Jeremiah or one of the prophets.' 'But you,' He asked them, 'who do you say that I am?' Simon Peter answered, 'You are the Messiah, the Son of the living God!'" (Matt. 16:13–16).

Some of His contemporaries imagined that Jesus was the second coming of John the Baptist, who had been beheaded by Herod for condemning Herod's adulterous relationship (Matt. 14:1–12). Others thought that Jesus was the reappearance of the prophet Elijah, who centuries earlier had been taken up into heaven on a chariot of fire in a whirlwind (2 Kings 2:1–14). Still others considered Jesus to be one of the great Old Testament prophets (like Isaiah or Jeremiah).

But all of these guesses were wrong. And (Simon) Peter, one of the twelve disciples, saw through all the confusion. He knew better because God had shown him the truth about his friend and Lord: Jesus was the long-awaited Messiah, God's chosen representative, the unique Son of God. At best, Peter partially understood what he had just announced about Jesus. Indeed, it would not be until after Jesus' crucifixion and resurrection that Peter would gain a good grasp of his own confession. For that matter, Peter would spend the rest of his life learning about Jesus.

Despite the incompleteness and tentativeness of his understanding, however, Peter did get it right: Jesus was the glorious, eternal Son of the living God—and He had become God's Man among men.

PAUSE TIME

"But You—Who Do You Say That I Am?" The same question resounds from the lips of Jesus Christ to His disciples today. Their names are no longer Simon Peter, James the son of Zebedee, Bartholomew, and Matthew the tax collector. Rather, they are Tasha, Megan, Whittannie, Jordan, Paige, Jason, Sydney—students like you. The question is a weighty one—in fact, it is the most important question in the universe! Your answer to it will determine your destiny—both in this life and for all eternity. If Jesus is nothing more than a fine ethical teacher or the founder

of a religion to you, please read on. If Jesus is far more important to you than a teacher or founder of a religion, or if
you just want to think about Him, keep reading to find out more
about Peter's reply: "You are the Messiah, the Son of the living God!"

CHAPTER TWO

THE GLORIOUS, ETERNAL SON OF GOD

Mark was causing trouble in our church. Apparently, he had made it known that he did not believe that Jesus Christ is God and saw himself on a special mission to straighten out others by helping them see that Jesus Christ is not God. So Mark engaged in conversations with people after church and even began to attend a Bible study where he could make his views known.

The leaders of my church requested that I talk with Mark. While the two of us met for several hours, I attempted to understand his idea of Jesus Christ. For Mark, Jesus is the greatest of created beings because He was the first of all created things and through Him God created all other existing things. Despite this lofty position, Mark explained, Jesus is still a created being; thus, He is not God.

Do you see any problems with Mark's view?

When I tried to discuss Scripture that affirms that Jesus Christ is God, Mark was ready with a different interpretation. When Mark pointed to other biblical passages that seemed to affirm that Jesus Christ is not God, I was ready with a different interpretation.

When I explained to Mark that his idea of Jesus Christ was first condemned as a wrong belief nearly seventeen hundred years ago (as early as AD 325), he informed me that the church had fallen into error on this matter within the first century of its existence.

I was perplexed. We had come to a standoff.

Then I opened up a critical issue. I asked Mark why he bothered coming to our church, given the fact that he considered it to be wrong on this issue of the deity of Jesus Christ. He explained that he was one of the chosen ones who knew the truth, and he was searching for others within our church whom he could lead out of error and into the truth about Jesus.

Mark then asked me why I was bothering to spend several hours with him discussing the deity of Jesus Christ. I paused, looked sadly yet urgently at him, and explained: "Your eternal salvation depends on this issue. If Jesus Christ is not truly God, as you believe, then He cannot save you. You are lost and condemned forever for rejecting Jesus Christ, our God and Savior."

As Mark looked at me in silence, I added, "And I will not allow you to recruit others in our church to your deceived idea that Jesus Christ is somehow less than God."

Mark got up and slowly walked away. I would never see him again.

Seeing Jesus As God

Though I have talked with many people about Jesus Christ, I must say that my conversation with Mark was one of the most frustrating and sad talks I have ever had. He was no demon with horns, no devil in disguise. On the contrary, he was a pleasant, friendly, intelligent guy who was wrong about the deity of Jesus Christ. But why was Mark wrong and what difference does it make anyway?

Try to imagine existence before the world came into being. No land, mountains, seas, earth, planets, solar system, Milky Way—no universe whatsoever. No presidents, kings, dictators, NBA/NFL/MLB/NHL players, school teachers, coaches, friends, family members—no you whatsoever. No animals, plants, viruses, microscopic creatures, chromosomes, DNA, hydrogen/oxygen/nitrogen/carbon—no life whatsoever.

No space.

No time.

No nothing.

With one exception: "The Word was with God, and the Word was God" (John 1:1).

We are told that there was One who existed before everything existed. John calls him the Word. He also is called the Son of God,

Immanuel (which means *God with us*), the Messiah, Savior, and Lord. We especially know Him by the name Jesus Christ.

The Preexistence of Jesus Christ

From the opening line of John's Gospel, we learn two things about the preexistence of the Word, Jesus Christ. First, "the Word was with God." He enjoyed a personal relationship with the Father. This means that He, the Son, is distinct from God the Father. Second, "the Word was God." He is divine. Though as the Son He is distinct from the Father, the Word is nevertheless fully God, sharing with the Father the very same divine attributes. There are no distinctions in the divine characteristics of the Father and of the Son. As the Father is present everywhere, sovereign, all-powerful, loving, all-knowing and wise, righteous, holy, merciful, gracious, jealous, wrathful, and so forth, so, too, is the Son.

Through this Word who was with God and was God, the entire universe and all that it contains came into existence: "All things were created through Him, and apart from Him not one thing was created that has been created" (John 1:3). This took place "in the beginning" (John 1:1).

If you read the first verse of Genesis, you will find the expression "in the beginning" as a reference to the event when "God created the heavens and the earth" (Gen. 1:1). Before this creation took place, "the Word was with God, and the Word was God." So we have the preexistent Word who was with God and was God before everything else that ever existed came into being.

This is confirmed elsewhere in Scripture:
He is the image of the invisible God,
the firstborn over all creation;
because *in* Him everything was created,
in heaven and on earth, the visible and the invisible,
whether thrones or dominions or rulers or authorities—
all things have been created through Him and for Him.
He is before all things, and *in* Him all things
    hold together.
(Col. 1:15–17, with my change of *in* for *by*)
In relationship to creation, Jesus Christ is the one *through whom* all things were created. This includes everything that exists in our

visible, material universe as well as everything that exists in the invisible, spiritual realm of angels, demons, and other supernatural realities. As God the Father was speaking the universe and all it contains into existence (Gen. 1), He created everything—light and darkness, the land and the water, fish and birds, plants and animals, human beings—through the agency of the Word.

Furthermore, Jesus Christ was the one *in whom* the Father's work of creation took place. As we will see, all of God's activity in our lives—from first designing us for a special relationship with Him, to bringing us into that relationship, and continuing until we live with Him forever—is done "in Christ." We can add to this God's work of creating the universe; the Father even accomplished that "in Christ."

In addition, Jesus Christ is the one *for whom* all things were created. He is the goal of all creation—the very reason for its existence—and God is working to sum up or "bring everything together" (Eph. 1:10) in Jesus Christ.

Given all of this, Jesus is rightly said to be *before all things*. Before all things were created, He already existed. Obviously, then, Jesus Christ was not created. So why is He given the title *the firstborn of all creation?* Doesn't this imply that He was created temporally like everything else? For example, my daughter Lauren is our firstborn because she was born before her sister and her brother. But this understanding of *firstborn*—that Jesus Christ was chronologically the first of all created beings—makes no sense with the explanation of this title in the rest of this passage.

The expression *firstborn* can also be a way of affirming that Jesus Christ is the supreme Lord over all creation. As the one *through whom* and *in whom* and *for whom* everything was created, Jesus Christ is preeminent over all creation. He is higher than every created thing. Furthermore, He is the one *in whom all things hold together.* Jesus Christ sustains the universe in existence. Indeed, apart from this constant sustaining activity, the universe and all that it contains would slip into oblivion and cease to be.

As the preexistent Word, what was existence like for the Son of God? We have already noted that He was fully God; indeed, Jesus Christ existed in the form of God, completely equal with the Father (Phil. 2:6). We also have seen that as the Son, He enjoyed a personal relationship with the Father. During His ministry on earth, Jesus uttered prayers that referred to the love and glory the Father and He shared from all eternity: "Father, I desire those You have given Me to be with Me where I am. Then they will see My glory, which You have given Me because You loved Me before the world's foundation" (John 17:24).

Before the universe came into existence—and with it, human beings to love—the Father and Son enjoyed a profound, eternal, dynamic, loving relationship. (We will see later that this loving community also included the Holy Spirit.) This love was expressed in the Father directing His majestic glory to be shared with the Son. Indeed, the Son "is the radiance of [the Father's] glory, the exact expression of His nature" (Heb. 1:3).

PAUSE TIME

As you reflect on the fact that Jesus Christ, the eternal Son of God, is the one *through whom* and *in whom* and *for whom* everything has been created, how does your perspective of Him change? How does the truth that you are created personally by Jesus Christ for His own purpose affect the plans and goals that you have or will set for yourself? If Jesus Christ is the perfect image of God, fully expressing the Father's glorious nature, then what could you do to know God and understand Him better?

Jesus Christ's Claims to Be God

When He became incarnate—when He took on human nature—the Son of God continued to express the fullness of deity as Jesus Christ, the God-man. For example, when His friend Philip requested that Jesus show the Father to the disciples to satisfy all their questions, Jesus replied: "Have I been among you all this time without your knowing Me, Philip? The one who has seen Me has seen the Father" (John 14:9).

This means that if we want to know what God the Father is like, we need only to look at Jesus Christ to see all that the Father is in visible form: "For in Him the entire fullness of God's nature dwells bodily" (Col. 2:9).

How it was possible for God to become a man will be the subject for a later chapter. But the Bible clearly shows that during His earthly ministry, Jesus Christ was fully conscious of being the God-man. In fact, even at an early age, He was aware of the unique relationship He enjoyed with the Father.

Every year His family traveled to Jerusalem to observe the Passover, an important Jewish celebration of God's delivering the Israelites out of slavery in Egypt. When Jesus was twelve years old, his parents began the long journey home from the Passover celebration in Jerusalem, unaware that Jesus was not traveling with them. Once they discovered Him missing, they returned to Jerusalem and searched for Him for three days, finally finding Him in the temple complex, deep in conversation with the religious teachers. "All those who heard Him were astounded at His understanding and His answers. When His parents saw Him, they were astonished, and His mother said to Him, 'Son, why have You treated us like this? Your father and I have been anxiously searching for You.' 'Why were you searching for Me?' He asked them. 'Didn't you know that I had to be in My Father's house?' But they did not understand what He said to them" (Luke 2:47–50). Even as a twelve-year-old, Jesus was conscious of a special relationship that He as the Son of God enjoyed with His Father.

Two decades later, as Jesus began His public ministry, this special status was publicly proclaimed (Mark 1:9–11): "In those days Jesus came from Nazareth in Galilee and was baptized in the Jordan by John. As soon as He came up out of the water, He saw the heavens being torn open and the Spirit descending to Him like a dove. And a voice came from heaven: 'You are My beloved Son; I take delight in You!'"

As this baptism unfolded, the Father Himself publicly acknowledged the unique relationship He enjoyed with His Son, Jesus Christ.

While some people of His time welcomed this specially selected Son of God, His unique relationship thrust Jesus into an adversarial position with the religious leaders. On one occasion, after teaching the crowds about the gift of eternal life and the care that the Father and He would take to protect His followers, Jesus explained, "'The Father and I are one.' Again the Jews picked up rocks to stone Him. Jesus replied, 'I have shown you many good works from the Father. Which of these works are you stoning Me for?' 'We aren't stoning You for a good work,' the Jews answered, 'but for blasphemy, and because You—being a man—make Yourself God'" (John 10:30–33).

Recognizing that Jesus was publicly affirming His equality with God, the religious leaders became angry, their bitterness reaching its climax at Jesus' trial where they confronted Him: "Then the high priest said to Him, 'By the living God I place You under oath: tell us if You are the Messiah, the Son of God!' 'You have said it,' Jesus told him. 'But I tell you, in the future you will see the Son of Man seated at the right hand of the Power, and coming on the clouds of heaven.' Then the high priest tore his robes and said, 'He has blasphemed! Why do we still need witnesses? Look, now you've heard the blasphemy! What is your decision?' They answered, 'He deserves death!'" (Matt. 26:63–66). The tearing of the high priest's robes was the customary action to indicate that blasphemy had been uttered—that a human being was claiming to be God. So incensed did the religious leaders become at Jesus that they made the final decision to send Him to His death. They would have nothing more to do with Jesus and His claims to be God.

PAUSE TIME

Did you ever read the gospel stories about Jesus and wonder why He didn't just go around telling everyone very clearly that He is God? Imagine this scenario of Jesus at a party, mingling and meeting people:

Tax collector: "Hey, I'm Zach the tax collector. Who are you?"

Jesus replies: "Hey, Zach, great to meet you. I'm Jesus. I'm God."

Prostitute: "I want to meet you. I'm Zenda the prostitute."

Jesus replies: "I've been wanting to meet you too, Zenda. My name is Jesus. I'm God."

If only Jesus had approached people this way—being very candid about being God—perhaps when we read the stories today, we would understand better Jesus' claims to be God.

But Jesus' approach—which seemed more hidden than open—was not a mistake on His part. He purposefully did not just come out and say He is God because His approach demanded that people

exercise faith to know His true identity. He didn't want mobs of
people clamoring after Him because they wanted some miracle of
food or healing or political freedom. That was not His purpose
at all.

Rather, He wanted followers who exercised a strong faith
and believed that He was much more than a mere man—even when
all the evidence pointed to Him being a mere man (like His sub-
mitting to torture and death). He wanted disciples who would
follow Him not because they marveled at His mighty miracles, but
because they were willing to sacrifice everything for His sake
whatever the cost.

Jesus did indeed make unmistakable claims to be God. No,
they don't sound like the claims someone today might use to
prove His deity. But Jesus' earthly ministry isn't taking place
today; He was here on earth two thousand years ago. And in
that time and place, Jesus made clear claims to be God. That's
precisely why His enemies wanted to kill Him.

The Miracles of Jesus Christ

It was one thing for Jesus to claim to be God. It was quite another thing for Him to support this claim, but that is exactly what
Jesus did. The miracles that typified His ministry were very powerful demonstrations of His identity as God.

On one occasion, Jesus and His disciples were traveling across
the Sea of Galilee. While Jesus was sleeping soundly, a fierce storm
arose and threatened to capsize their vulnerable fishing boat. And
being aroused, "He got up and rebuked the wind and the surging
waves, and they stopped, and it became calm. And He said to them,
'Where is your faith?' They were fearful and amazed, saying to one
another, 'Who then is this, that He commands even the winds
and the water, and they obey Him?'" (Luke 8:24–25 NASB). On
this and other occasions, Jesus clearly demonstrated His identity
as God through His miraculous control over the powerful forces
of nature.

Many times Jesus encountered sick, deformed, and handi-
capped people. "When Jesus went into Peter's house, He saw his
mother-in-law lying in bed with a fever. So He touched her hand,
and the fever left her. Then she got up and began to serve Him"
(Matt. 8:14–15). Jesus healed others who had been deformed from
birth—the mute who had never spoken, the deaf who had never

heard a sound, the lame who had never walked, and, as in the following example, the blind who had never seen. "As He was passing by, He saw a man blind from birth. . . . He spit on the ground, made some mud from the saliva, and spread the mud on his eyes. 'Go,' He told him, 'wash in the pool of Siloam' (which means 'Sent'). So he left, washed, and came back seeing" (John 9:1, 6–7).

On another occasion, "A woman suffering from bleeding for twelve years had endured much under many doctors. She had spent everything she had, and was not helped at all. On the contrary, she became worse. Having heard about Jesus, she came behind Him in the crowd and touched His robe. For she said, 'If I can just touch His robes, I'll be made well!' Instantly her flow of blood ceased, and she sensed in her body that she was cured of her affliction" (Mark 5:25–29).

Jesus clearly demonstrated His identity as God by miraculously curing these people.

Still others were under nearly constant attack from demons who possessed them and caused tragic suffering. Listen to the description of one demon-possessed man:

When [Jesus] got out on land, a demon-possessed man from the town met Him. For a long time he had worn no clothes and did not stay in a house but in the tombs. When he saw Jesus, he cried out, fell down before Him, and said in a loud voice, "What do You have to do with me, Jesus, You Son of the Most High God? I beg You, don't torment me!" For He had commanded the unclean spirit to come out of the man. Many times it had seized him, and although he was guarded, bound by chains and shackles, he would snap the restraints and be driven by the demon into deserted places. (Luke 8:27–29)

Jesus cast out the demons. When the crowd came to see what had happened, they "found the man the demons had departed from, sitting at Jesus' feet, dressed and in his right mind" (Luke 8:35). Jesus clearly demonstrated His identity as God by miraculously casting out demons.

On still other occasions, Jesus came face-to-face with death itself. Even when confronted with this heartbreaking and seemingly irreversible event, Jesus worked miraculously: "Just as He neared the gate of the town, a dead man was being carried out. He was his mother's only son, and she was a widow. A large crowd from the city was also with her. When the Lord saw her, He had compassion on her and said, 'Don't cry!' Then He came up and touched the open coffin, and the pallbearers stopped. And He said, 'Young man, I tell you, get up!' The dead man sat up and began to speak, and Jesus gave him to his mother" (Luke 7:12–15).

As might be expected, the response of the crowd was amazement: "Then fear came over everyone, and they glorified God, saying, 'A great prophet has risen among us,' and 'God has visited His people'" (Luke 7:16). Jesus clearly demonstrated His identity as God by miraculously raising people from the dead.

He exercised powerful control over the forces of nature, healed the sick and deformed, exorcised demons, and raised the dead. On the one hand, these miraculous demonstrations of Jesus' identity as God were unusual in that people who witnessed them were undoubtedly surprised, even frightened. On the other hand, these miracles were a common element of Jesus' ministry: "Jesus was going all over Galilee, teaching in their synagogues, preaching the good news of the kingdom, and healing every disease and sickness among the people. Then the news about Him spread throughout Syria. So they brought to Him all those who were afflicted, those suffering from various diseases and intense pains, the demon-possessed, the epileptics, and the paralytics. And He healed them" (Matt. 4:23–24). Many people who witnessed these miracles responded to them by following Jesus. They recognized that no mere human being could do the things Jesus did. His miracles were clear demonstrations of His identity as God.

PAUSE TIME

As you read these and other stories about Jesus' miracles, ask yourself if there is anything in this life—sickness, disease, demonic power, impending death—that is outside of Jesus' control. How does your answer encourage you to look at Jesus?

Two other miracles demand our attention. As we have seen, God the Son participated actively in the creation of the universe.

As the Son of God incarnate, Jesus Christ performed another miracle of creation when He provided food for thousands of people who had gathered to hear His teaching and receive His healing.

> When evening came, the disciples approached Him and said, "This place is a wilderness, and it is already late. Send the crowds away so they can go into the villages and buy food for themselves." "They don't need to go away," Jesus told them. "You give them something to eat." "But we only have five loaves and two fish here," they said to Him. "Bring them here to Me," He said. Then He commanded the crowds to sit down on the grass. He took the five loaves and the two fish, and looking up to heaven, He blessed them. He broke the loaves and gave them to the disciples, and the disciples [gave them] to the crowds. Everyone ate and was filled. Then they picked up twelve baskets full of leftover pieces! Now those who ate were about five thousand men, besides women and children. (Matt. 14:15–21)

Filled with compassion for those whom He had taught and healed, Jesus performed a miracle of creation. He multiplied a few loaves of bread and some fish so that fifteen thousand or more people would have the necessary provisions for their evening meal. The plight of the twelve disciples, who were helpless to do anything other than send away the people to fend for themselves, underscores the impotency of human resources. What a contrast between human weakness and the overabundant resources of the God-man Jesus Christ!

So that we do not fix our attention solely on the physical awesomeness of Jesus' miracles, a final healing miracle of physical and spiritual ailments demands our attention. On an occasion of Jesus' teaching in His hometown, four friends dug a hole in the roof of the house where He was teaching and lowered a bed carrying a paralytic.

> Seeing their faith, Jesus told the paralytic, "Son, your sins are forgiven." But some of the scribes were sitting there, thinking to themselves: "Why does He speak like this? He's blaspheming! Who can forgive sins but God alone?" Right away Jesus understood in His spirit that

they were reasoning like this within themselves and said
to them, "Why are you reasoning these things in your
hearts? Which is easier: to say to the paralytic, 'Your sins
are forgiven,' or to say, 'Get up, pick up your stretcher,
and walk'? But so you may know that the Son of Man
has authority on earth to forgive sins," He told the paralytic, "I tell you: get up, pick up your stretcher, and go
home." Immediately he got up, picked up the stretcher,
and went out in front of everyone. As a result, they were
all astonished and gave glory to God, saying, "We have
never seen anything like this!" (Mark 2:5–12)

Obviously, it was easier for Jesus to say that the paralytic's sins were
forgiven; nothing could prove such a statement to be wrong (or, for
that matter, affirm it to be true). But Jesus performed the miracle
of healing specifically to prove His own authority to forgive the sins
of the paralytic (and any other person as well). As His opponents
so rightly stated, no one but God has such authority. Jesus' miracle
attested to the fact that He is God.

Jesus claimed to be God.

He supported His claims with miracles.

PAUSE TIME

Do you believe the claim of Jesus Christ: that He is fully God?
How do His miracles help you in this? As you consider the different types of miracles—controlling the forces of nature,
healing the sick and deformed, exorcising demons, and raising the dead—are you encouraged to trust Jesus Christ with
the difficult situations you face in life today? How might the
reality of Jesus' identity as God help you with problems with
your parents and family, relationship difficulties with friends
and classmates, frustrations and discouragements at church and
school, and overall disappointments with yourself?

The Deity of Jesus: Errors to Avoid

And so we are to embrace Jesus as being fully God. On two
occasions, the New Testament writers describe Him as "our great
God and Savior, Christ Jesus" (Titus 2:13; 2 Pet. 1:1). Indeed, to
deny the identity of Jesus as God is to commit a grave error.

So how would you reply if one of your friends said he believed that Jesus was only a man whom God adopted as His Son? Or what would you say if one of your friends decided that Jesus was only a created being—the highest and most important created being, but a created being nonetheless?

These two views are erroneous. *Adoptionism* believes that God adopted the man Jesus as His Son. Supposedly, this took place at His baptism, when the presence and power of God came upon Jesus and He was proclaimed to be the Father's Son. This belief assumes that at His crucifixion, when Jesus cried out, "My God, My God, why have You forsaken Me?" (Matt. 27:46), this divine presence departed from Jesus. So Jesus was not God who became man, but merely a man in whom God was peculiarly and powerfully active. Thus, adoptionism denies that Jesus is Himself God.

Arianism is a view named for a man who lived in the fourth century, about three hundred years after Christ. Arius believed that Jesus was the one through whom every created thing in the universe came into existence. The heavens and earth, light and darkness, the sea and the land, plants and animals, angels and human beings—everything was created through Him and for Him. However, this belief holds that Jesus Himself was a created being. He was created before everything else as the highest creature, but He was created. Arius believed that there was a time when the Son of God did not exist, which denies Christ's eternal nature. And Arius believed that the Son of God was of a different nature from God the Father; that is, He is not fully God.

As Arius was communicating his beliefs, many church leaders met together and decided that Arianism was absolutely false. They affirmed the belief that the Son of God has the same nature as God the Father, that He is eternal, and that He is not a created being.[1] From that time on, the church has always believed that Jesus Christ is fully God and has condemned those who hold to Arianism. Today, many non-Christian groups—cults like Jehovah's Witnesses and Mormons—hold to a form of Arianism. Mark, whose story I told at the beginning of this chapter, held to Arianism. Understanding these views helps us make clear distinctions between Christian and non-Christian beliefs, so that we are not taken unaware by twists on the truth of Christ.

PAUSE TIME

Do you know people who deny that Jesus Christ is fully God? Do
they believe that Jesus just had the power of God working in
Him? Do they believe that Jesus is the most awesome of created
beings but still something less than God? What could you share
from this chapter that might help them realize their error
about Jesus Christ?

CHAPTER THREE

A REAL AND FULLY HUMAN BEING

My wife and I used to be staff members of Campus Crusade for Christ. For several years we had the opportunity to work in contexts that were predominately Roman Catholic—the University of Notre Dame and Rome, Italy. On occasion, Notre Dame students and Italians would ask us, "Why don't you pray to Mary? We Catholics do, but you Protestants don't pray to her. Why is this?" Inevitably, our answer would revolve around a particular biblical passage that speaks about Jesus: "Since we have a great high priest who has passed through the heavens—Jesus the Son of God—let us hold fast to the confession. For we do not have a high priest who is unable to sympathize with our weaknesses, but One who has been tested in every way as we are, yet without sin. Therefore, let us approach the throne of grace with boldness, so that we may receive mercy and find grace to help us at the proper time" (Heb. 4:14–16).

As we would explain to our Catholic friends, the Bible affirms that Jesus Christ was fully human. During His earthly ministry as our High Priest (the one who stands between us and God to bring us back into a relationship with God), Jesus endured all the same temptations and trials that we face, being fully human as we are. Because of these common human experiences, Jesus understands us completely and sympathizes with us as we struggle against sin and suffering. He knows what we are going through because He went through the very same difficulties.

Despite this biblical emphasis, the Catholic church has tended to minimize or overlook the real humanity of Jesus. By emphasizing His deity, Catholics have rightly insisted that Jesus is God, but in a way that makes Jesus seem very remote from the rest of us. To bridge this chasm between Jesus and us, the Catholic church offers Mary because (1) as a human being like us, she can relate to the difficulties we go through, and (2) as the mother of Jesus, she can direct His attention toward us so that He will help us in our struggles. For these reasons, Catholics pray to Mary.

However, as the Bible affirms, because Jesus was fully human, *He* can already relate to us and help us as we face temptations and trials. We can go directly to Him in prayer without a mediator like Mary between Jesus and us. In fact, at no point in Scripture is Mary given any qualities of serving as our savior or our interceder between us and God. Jesus, however, is named as both: "Therefore he is able to save completely those who come to God through him, because he always lives to intercede for them" (Heb. 7:25 NIV).

Back to our point of Jesus empathizing with our trials: such understanding hinges on seeing Jesus as a real and fully human being.

Seeing Jesus as Man

Have you ever considered the fact that Jesus was a real flesh-and-blood person, fully human just like you and me? At times, we may so focus on seeing Jesus as God that it's difficult to see Him as a man. We lose sight of His full humanity—a dangerous and tragic thing to do.

The Birth and Childhood of Jesus

The Bible clearly and consistently affirms that Jesus Christ was a real and fully human being. His birth was normal in every way, presented with amazing simplicity. While Joseph and Mary were in Bethlehem, "it happened that the days were completed for her to give birth. Then she gave birth to her firstborn Son, and she wrapped Him snugly in cloth and laid Him in a manger—because there was no room for them at the inn" (Luke 2:6–7).

Though the Christmas carol imagines "the little Lord Jesus, no crying He makes," Jesus undoubtedly fussed and wailed when

He was hungry or needed a diaper change. Also, His development from infancy to adulthood was normal in every way, encompassing intellectual, physical, spiritual, and social growth: "And Jesus increased in wisdom and stature, and in favor with God and with people" (Luke 2:52).

As a boy, Jesus probably studied the trade of carpentry from His father, Joseph; learned several languages (His first language was Aramaic, along with Hebrew and probably Greek); memorized Scripture (the Hebrew Bible—what Christians call the Old Testament); and made yearly trips to the temple along with His family (Luke 2:41–51).

PAUSE TIME

Something was peculiar about how Jesus came into existence. Though we Christians commonly refer to it as the "virgin birth," a more accurate phrase to describe this miraculous event would be the "virgin conception." That is, the birth of Jesus was normal in every way (as noted above), but His conception was miraculous. In either case, we mean that Mary was a virgin when Jesus was conceived in her womb. The Gospel of Matthew relates part of the story:

> The birth of Jesus Christ came about this way: After His mother Mary had been engaged to Joseph, it was discovered before they came together that she was pregnant by the Holy Spirit. So her husband Joseph, being a righteous man, and not wanting to disgrace her publicly, decided to divorce her secretly.
>
> But after he had considered these things, an angel of the Lord suddenly appeared to him in a dream, saying, "Joseph, son of David, don't be afraid to take Mary as your wife, because what has been conceived in her is by the Holy Spirit. She will give birth to a son, and you are to name Him Jesus; because He will save His people from their sins." Now all this took place to fulfill what was spoken by the Lord through the prophet [Isaiah 7:14]: "See, the virgin will become pregnant and give birth to a son, and they will name Him Immanuel, which is translated 'God is with us.'"
>
> When Joseph got up from sleeping, he did as the Lord's angel had commanded him. He married her but did not know her intimately until she gave birth to a son. And he named Him Jesus. (Matt. 1:18-25)

The Gospel of Luke relates the conversation between the angel Gabriel and Mary concerning her conception of Jesus:

> In the sixth month [of Elizabeth's pregnancy], the angel Gabriel was sent by God to a town in Galilee called Nazareth, to a virgin engaged to a man named Joseph, of the house of David. The virgin's name was Mary. And [the angel] came to her and said, "Rejoice, favored woman! The Lord is with you." But she was deeply troubled by this statement, wondering what kind of greeting this could be. Then the angel told her,
>
> "Do not be afraid, Mary, for you have found favor with God. Now listen: You will conceive and give birth to a son, and you will call His name JESUS. He will be great and will be called the Son of the Most High, and the Lord God will give Him the throne of His father David. He will reign over the house of Jacob forever, and His kingdom will have no end."
>
> Mary asked the angel, "How can this be, since I have not been intimate with a man?"
>
> The angel replied to her: "The Holy Spirit will come upon you, and the power of the Most High will overshadow you. Therefore the holy One to be born will be called the Son of God." (Luke 1:26-35)

Jesus was not conceived through an act of sexual intercourse between His mother, Mary, and Joseph, the man to whom she was engaged to be married. She was a virgin, never having been physically intimate with her fiancé. Rather, the Holy Spirit powerfully overshadowed Mary and brought about the conception of Jesus in her womb. This was a unique and miraculous event, beginning the earthly term of the Son of God in the human form of Jesus Christ. Thus, we affirm that Jesus was "born of the virgin Mary."[2]

The Earthly Ministry of Jesus

As He engaged in His three-year ministry, Jesus continued to live as a real and fully human being. We see Him hungry and needing to eat food to nourish His body, especially after fasting forty days and nights in the wilderness (Matt. 4:1-2). He was thirsty and so drank water to quench his thirst, as when a weary Jesus asked the woman of Samaria to give Him some water from her well (John 4:6-7). We find Him tired and sleeping soundly, as when Jesus slept peacefully during a violent windstorm that threatened to sink the boat in which He and His disciples were traveling (Matt. 8:23–27).

Furthermore, He needed alone time, periodically retreating from His exhausting ministry to the crowds to be alone. For example, when Jesus heard of the death of John the Baptist, "He withdrew from there by boat to a remote place to be alone" (Matt. 14:13). And after He miraculously fed the five thousand, Jesus dispersed the crowds and "went up on the mountain by Himself to pray. When evening came, He was there alone" (Matt. 14: 23). Besides engaging in personal prayer to the Father (Luke 6:12), Jesus also attended His local synagogue (Luke 4:16), where He worshipped God along with others and strengthened His relationship with the Father.

During His ministry, Jesus developed and enjoyed close friendships with His disciples and others. His disciple John was known as the disciple "Jesus loved" (John 13:23; 20:2). Peter, James, and John—who formed the inner circle of His twelve disciples— were with Him at critical moments in His life (at the transfiguration [Matt. 17:1–9] and in the garden of Gethsemane [Mark 14:32–42]).

Of course, Jesus spent almost the entirety of His ministry with the twelve disciples, teaching and training them. Yet His friendships were not reserved for these men alone: As Jesus traveled about, "the Twelve were with Him, and also some women who had been healed of evil spirits and sicknesses: Mary, called Magdalene (seven demons had come out of her); Joanna the wife of Chuza, Herod's steward; Susanna; and many others who were supporting them from their possessions" (Luke 8:1–3). Moreover, "Jesus loved Martha, her sister [Mary], and Lazarus" (John 11:5)—so much so that when Lazarus died, Jesus wept while others exclaimed, "See how He loved him!" (John 11:35–36).

Jesus' friendships extended far beyond the cast of characters we normally associate with Him. A frequent participant at parties attended by the people society despised, Jesus Himself noted: "The Son of Man came eating and drinking, and they say, 'Look, a glutton [one who eats far too much] and a drunkard, a friend of tax collectors and sinners!'" (Matt. 11:19).

Beyond this deep love that bound Him to His friends, Jesus was often moved with compassion for people He had just "randomly" met. When a man who suffered from leprosy (a dreadful disease that eats away holes in a person's skin) begged Jesus to make his disintegrating body whole again, "moved with compassion, Jesus reached out His hand and touched him. 'I am willing,' He told him. 'Be made clean.' Immediately the disease left him, and he was healed" (Mark 1:41–42). Can you imagine the response of this leper to his healing?!

When two blind men, hearing that Jesus was passing by, cried out loudly to Him to have mercy on them, "Jesus stopped, called, them, and said, 'What do you want Me to do for you?' 'Lord,' they said to Him, 'open our eyes!' Moved with compassion, Jesus touched their eyes. Immediately they could see, and they followed Him" (Matt. 20:32–34). Can you imagine the response of these blind men to their healing?!

Jesus' compassion extended to those who had suffered great loss, as in the case of a widow whose only son had died. "When the Lord saw her, He had compassion on her and said, 'Don't cry.' Then He came up and touched the open coffin, and the pallbearers stopped. And He said, 'Young man, I tell you, get up!' The dead man sat up and began to speak, and Jesus gave him to his mother" (Luke 7:13–15). Can you imagine the response of this widow to her dead son's new life?!

Jesus was stirred by this same compassion for the untold number of tired and directionless people who followed Him: "When He saw the crowds, He felt compassion for them, because they were weary and worn out, like sheep without a shepherd" (Matt. 9:36). Jesus was full of compassion for people He had never met.

PAUSE TIME

You've probably had someone in your church remind you that Christians are to be "in the world but not of the world" (Jesus teaches on this in John 17). You've also probably been warned to "not be yoked together with unbelievers" (2 Cor. 6:14 NIV). At times, this counsel almost sounds as though we are to have no relationships whatsoever with people who don't know Jesus Christ. But how does Jesus and the variety of the friendships He enjoyed help us be His followers in the world without succumbing to the temptations and sins of the world?

Toward those who did not feel compassion in the face of suffering and need, Jesus expressed disappointment, anger, and indignation. One Sabbath, the religious critics waited in the wings to see if Jesus would heal a man with a paralyzed hand. (By doing so, Jesus would break their rule of not doing any work on the Sabbath, or day of rest, and they could accuse Him of wrongdoing. Remember: all Jesus wanted to do was restore the man's hand!) Jesus "told the man with the paralyzed hand, 'Stand before us.' Then He said to them [His critics], 'Is it lawful on the Sabbath to do good or to do evil, to save life or to kill?' But they were silent. After looking around at them with anger and sorrow at the hardness of their hearts, He told the man, 'Stretch out your hand.' So he stretched it out, and his hand was restored" (Mark 3:3–5).

How could these critics be so cold, so hardened they could not see beyond their own religious rules and traditions to relieve the man's suffering? Jesus was filled with anger at their lack of compassion.

With similar all-consuming emotion, Jesus lashed out at the businessmen and bankers who had transformed the temple from the center of worship to a commercial mall. "After making a whip out of cords, He drove everyone out of the temple complex with their sheep and oxen. He also poured out the money changers' coins and overturned the tables. He told those who were selling doves, 'Get these things out of here! Stop turning My Father's house into a marketplace!' And His disciples remembered that it is written: 'Zeal for Your house will consume Me'" (John 2:15–17).

Jesus was equally indignant in the face of another evil—this time, however, His anger seethed not at people but at death itself. He arrived at the grave of His friend Lazarus and was struck by the sorrow of the situation. "When Jesus saw [Mary] crying, and the Jews who had come with her crying, He was angry in His spirit and deeply moved" (John 11:33).

Jesus was embittered at death, the great and unmerciful enemy of people whom He loved. "The spectacle of the distress of Mary and her companions enraged Jesus because it brought poignantly home to His consciousness the evil of death, its unnaturalness, its 'violent tyranny.' . . . It is death that is the object of His wrath, and behind death him who has the power of death, and whom He has come into the world to destroy."[3]

Though we often (and rightly) imagine Jesus as deeply disturbed by the suffering and evil in the world, we should not think of Him only as "a man of sorrows" (Isa. 53:3 NIV). Intermixed with His difficulties and the oppression He had to shoulder was joy. "He rejoiced greatly in the Holy Spirit" (Luke 10:21 NASB) at the progress of the kingdom of God through His ministry.

When a centurion, who had no business understanding the ways of Jesus, expressed faith that Jesus could heal his paralyzed servant by the mere utterance of a word, "Jesus was amazed and said to those following Him, 'I assure you: I have not found anyone in Israel with so great a faith!'" (Matt. 8:10). No wonder we are commanded to keep "our eyes on Jesus, the source and perfecter of our faith, who *for the joy that lay before Him* endured a cross and despised the shame" (Heb. 12:2).

In the Shadow of the Cross

Jesus' life was lived in the dreadful shadow of the cross. He was fully aware of the excruciating physical pain and the searing separation from the Father that awaited Him at the completion of His ministry. Yet this did not cause Jesus to shrink back. On the contrary, He relentlessly pursued His mission, proclaiming, "I came to bring fire on the earth, and how I wish it were already ablaze! But I have a baptism to be baptized with [a veiled reference to His impending death], and how it consumes Me until it is finished!" (Luke 12:49–50). He set a course resolutely for Jerusalem, where He would meet His tragic yet necessary death. Indeed, Jesus often predicted His death with alarmingly painful precision: "While going up to Jerusalem, Jesus took the twelve disciples aside privately and said to them on the way: 'Listen! We are going up to Jerusalem. The Son of Man will be handed over to the chief priests and scribes, and they will condemn Him to death. Then they will hand Him over to the Gentiles to be mocked, flogged, and crucified, and He will be resurrected on the third day'" (Matt. 20:17–19).

As the time of His death drew closer, Jesus felt more and more distressed by its wretched prospects. "Now My soul is troubled. What should I say—'Father, save Me from this hour?' But that is why I came to this hour" (John 12:27). And so in the garden of Gethsemane, Jesus wrestled intensely with the choice of death or life:

Then they came to a place named Gethsemane, and He told His disciples, "Sit here while I pray." He took Peter, James, and John with Him, and He began to be deeply distressed and horrified. Then He said to them, "My soul is swallowed up in sorrow—to the point of death. Remain here and stay awake." Then He went a little farther, fell to the ground, and began to pray that if it were possible, the hour might pass from Him. And He said, "Abba, Father! All things are possible for You. Take this cup away from Me. Nevertheless, not what I will, but what You will." (Mark 14:32–36)

The drama of Jesus' wrestling with death and life—the will of His Father versus His own will—highlights the true humanity of Jesus. He was no divine being slipping through the long and painful race of life with privileged treatment and an easily won place of honor at the finish line. Like every other human being, Jesus had to endure temptation and trial, leaning on the Father for strength and rescue every step of the way. "During His earthly life, He offered prayers and appeals, with loud cries and tears, to the One who was able to save Him from death, and He was heard because of His reverence. Though a Son, He learned obedience through what He suffered" (Heb. 5:7–8).

By bearing up under the pressures and pains of life, Jesus became perfectly fitted to be our Savior. In consistently abiding by the Father's will throughout all the challenges of trials and temptations of His life, Jesus was well prepared to face the ultimate challenge—laying down His life to die a death on a cross—at His life's end. Only a perfect human being could save us by sacrificing His own life for us, and so "He became the source of eternal salvation to all who obey Him" (Heb. 5:9).

Jesus' Trials and Temptations

Throughout His life, Jesus continually faced temptations and trials as do all other human beings—like you and me. Though we often think of Jesus' sufferings as being confined to His crucifixion and the torture He endured in the hours leading up to that event, such assumptions are inaccurate. From the outset of His ministry, He came face-to-face with temptations and troubles of all types.

The most noted of these, of course, were the temptations He encountered in the wilderness at the hands of Satan (Matt. 4:1–11).
The tempter encouraged Jesus to take the easy way out of difficulty
and enticed Him with the promise of power, fame, and privilege.
But these struggles were just the beginning of a ministry fraught
with difficulties.

Imagine what it must have been like for Jesus to attempt to
mentor and teach His disciples on a daily basis, only for them to
misunderstand and fail Him time and again. For example, shortly
after His marvelous recognition of Jesus as "the Messiah, the Son
of the living God!" (Matt. 16:16), Peter took Jesus aside and rebuked Him for predicting His upcoming death and resurrection.
Jesus' response put Peter into his place: "Get behind Me, Satan!
You are an offense to Me because you're not thinking about God's
concerns, but man's" (Matt. 16:23).

On another occasion, Peter courageously obeyed the command
of Jesus to walk on the water toward Him. "But when [Peter] saw
the strength of the wind, he was afraid. And beginning to sink he
cried out, 'Lord, save me!' Immediately Jesus reached out His hand,
caught hold of him, and said to him, 'You of little faith, why did
you doubt?'" (Matt. 14:30–31).

Of course, Peter was not alone in his bumbling misunderstanding of Jesus. All twelve disciples joined in to disappoint and
frustrate Jesus. Though they had participated in Jesus' feeding of
five thousand people one time and in His feeding of four thousand
people another time, the disciples did not grasp the miraculous
resourcefulness of Jesus to provide food when an insufficient
quantity was to be found. So when Jesus warned them about the
"yeast" of the religious leaders, their response was an embarrassing
concern that they had forgotten to bring bread with them for the
trip. Once again, Jesus scolded them, reminding them of what they
had seen and experienced but failed to internalize:

> "Why are you discussing that you do not have any
> bread? Do you not yet understand or comprehend? Is
> your heart hardened? Do you have eyes, and not see,
> and do you have ears, and not hear? And do you not re-
> member? When I broke the five loaves for the 5,000, how
> many baskets full of pieces of bread did you collect?"

"Twelve," they told Him.
"When I broke the seven loaves for the 4,000, how many large baskets full of pieces of bread did you collect?"
"Seven," they said. (Mark 8:17–20)
The disciples, often focused on their own aspirations or physical needs, failed to see that Jesus was talking figuratively about false teaching (yeast was a common metaphor for error), not bread. They had already forgotten His ability to provide plentiful food for huge crowds of hungry people. How Jesus' frustration with His disciples deepened! Indeed, they never did grasp who Jesus truly was during His earthly ministry.

As if this were not enough, Jesus also ran into misunderstandings with His own family. Not only did they doubt Him—"for not even His brothers believed in Him" (John 7:5)—but they also wanted to restrain and even take Jesus into their custody "because they said, 'He's out of His mind'" (Mark 3:21). Many of the Jews took a similarly insulting stance on Him, saying, "He has a demon and He's crazy!" (John 10:20). So in addition to being considered insane, Jesus also was accused of being demon-possessed.

But Jesus' enemies did not stop with verbal accusations. Their contempt for Him spilled over into attempts to kill Him. On one occasion, Jesus challenged the people in His synagogue to recognize the work of God. "When they heard this, everyone in the synagogue was enraged. They got up, drove Him out of town, and brought Him to the edge of the hill their town was built on, intending to hurl Him over the cliff. But He passed right through the crowd and went on His way" (Luke 4:28–30).

As the ministry of Jesus progressed, His enemies sought to execute Jesus on various occasions, often in response to His veiled claims that He was indeed God. For example, after Jesus indicated that He existed (as God) prior to the time of Abraham (who lived more than two millennia before Jesus was born), "they picked up stones to throw at Him. But Jesus was hidden and went out of the temple complex" (John 8:59). Not long after this incident, Jesus stated, "'The Father and I are one.' Again the Jews picked up rocks to stone Him. Jesus replied, 'I have shown you many good works from the Father. Which of these works are you stoning Me for?' 'We aren't stoning You for a good work,' the Jews answered, 'but for blasphemy, and because You—being a man—make Yourself God'" (John 10:30–33).

Though each of these attempts to kill Jesus failed, ultimately He was betrayed by His disciple Judas, brought to trial, falsely accused, convicted though innocent, and executed by means of crucifixion.

Tempted to take the easy way out of difficulty. Enticed with the promise of power, fame, and privilege. Miserably misunderstood even by His closest friends. Considered crazy by His own family. Accused of being demon-possessed by His enemies. Charged with blasphemy and targeted for stoning by His religious critics. Betrayed by someone He loved. Wrongly accused and convicted. Crucified though innocent. Was Jesus tempted and distressed by the same temptations and troubles that we face? Absolutely! We face nothing that Jesus did not have to face as well.

PAUSE TIME

So here is a question to ponder: What is the most difficult situation in your life right now? Are friends misunderstanding you? Is your family underestimating you? Have you been betrayed? Falsely slandered? Is a huge temptation looming large before your eyes? Now consider the fact that Jesus faced the very same temptations and troubles. He can sympathize with your plight. He has been where you are now. He knows how you feel. And He is able to come to your aid so that you can do the right thing in the midst of your temptation or trial. "For since He Himself was tested and has suffered, He is able to help those who are tested" (Heb. 2:18). Run to Jesus and find help for yourself!

The Sinlessness of Jesus

Wait a minute! What was it that I just wrote? Jesus is able to help "so that you can *do the right thing* in the midst of your temptation or trial." We are so accustomed to falling short or failing when troubled or tempted that we almost never consider that Jesus can enable us to overcome the temptations or to respond well in our troubles. But that is the reality of living with Jesus—a real and fully human being who never once sinned. Over and over again, the Bible describes Jesus as "the One who did not know sin" (2 Cor.

5:21), "holy, innocent, undefiled, separated from sinners" (Heb. 7:26), "One who has been tested in every way as we are, yet without sin" (Heb. 4:15). As such, Jesus becomes our example to follow when we face trials and suffering—we are to avoid sinning and do right, even as Jesus did:

For you were called to this,
because Christ also suffered for you,
leaving you an example,
so that you should follow in His steps.
He did not commit sin,
and no deceit was found in His mouth;
when reviled, He did not revile in return;
when suffering, He did not threaten,
but committed Himself to the One who judges justly.
(1 Pet. 2:21-23)

Rather than lashing out angrily at those who cause us trouble, rather than taking matters into our own hands, we are to entrust ourselves to God and continue to act in ways that please Him. After all, "you know that [Jesus] was revealed so that He might take away sins, and there is no sin in Him. Everyone who remains in Him does not sin; everyone who sins has not seen Him or known Him" (1 John 3:5-6). The key to pleasing God when we face temptations and undergo trials is to remain strongly attached to Jesus and rely upon His strength to overcome. Although everything in our being screams to just give up and fail, we must remember that we do not need to fall. We do not have to sin—ever. Don't believe the lie that sin is inevitable. There is always another choice. Jesus, a real and fully human being like we are, never once sinned. We do not have to sin either. After all, "God is faithful and He will not allow you to be tempted beyond what you are able, but with the temptation He will also provide a way of escape, so that you are able to bear it" (1 Cor. 10:13).

PAUSE TIME

But didn't Jesus have an unfair advantage over us because, in addition to being a human being, He was also God? Wasn't it easy for Him because, when fiercely tempted and troubled, He could just fall back on His divine nature so as to be kept from sinning?

I grant that it could have been like that for Jesus; indeed, I might even say that His divine nature would have necessarily prevented Jesus from ever sinning. But the Bible does not picture Jesus living like that. What did He do when facing Satan's temptations in the wilderness? Jesus depended on the Word of God to stave off the enticements to power, fame, and privilege. What did He do when facing the ultimate choice to do the Father's will and die by crucifixion or to follow His own will and avoid dying on the cross? Jesus fervently prayed and relied on the Father's strength to will the right choice. It was never easy for Jesus to avoid sinning.

As human beings ourselves, we know that fleeing from temptation and holding up under suffering is never easy! Yet, Jesus never once sinned—not because He took the easy way out by relying on His divine nature (a divine nature that we do not possess), but because He resolutely purposed to accomplish the Father's will according to the Word of God and, praying, relied on the Father's strength to overcome temptation and trial. As human beings, can we not do the very same? WWJD? Holding on to Scripture, praying, and relying on God's strength enables us to do what Jesus did.

But what about all the times we do fail—not inevitably, but realistically speaking? As we have already seen, Jesus "was revealed so that He might take away sins" (1 John 3:5). The reason the Son of God became incarnate as Jesus Christ was to deal with our sins through atonement and forgiveness (more about this later). When—not if—we fall and sin, "if we confess our sins, He is faithful and righteous to forgive us our sins and to cleanse us from all unrighteousness" (1 John 1:9). Jesus offers forgiveness and cleansing from every fall into temptation and from every failure in the midst of trial and trouble.

The Humanity of Jesus: Errors to Avoid

And so we are to embrace Jesus as a real and fully human being. "The Word became flesh and took up residence among us. We observed His glory, the glory as the One and Only Son from the Father, full of grace and truth" (John 1:14). Indeed, to deny the humanity of Jesus is to commit a grave error: "This is how you know the Spirit of God: Every spirit who confesses that Jesus Christ has come in the flesh is from God. But every spirit who does not confess Jesus is not from God. This is the spirit of the antichrist" (1 John 4:2-3).

So how would you respond if a friend said that Jesus was not a real and fully human being? Perhaps your friend believes that Jesus was not human at all, or that Jesus was only partially human. Would this trouble you? Why? What would you say if your friend believed that Jesus' humanity was completely irrelevant?

Numerous erroneous views exist on Christ's humanity. *Docetism* (from a Greek word that means *to appear* or *to seem*) believes that Jesus only appeared or seemed to be human. His physical existence was an illusion, an apparition. At the heart of this view is the belief that material reality—our physical body, for example—is inherently evil. The implication of this belief is that the Son of God could never have taken on human nature because it is wicked and sinful. Thus, docetism denies the real humanity of Jesus.

The *partial humanity view*[4] believes that Jesus took on genuine human nature but not a complete human nature. He possessed a real human body but lacked a human soul. At the heart of this view is the belief that if the Son of God took on full human nature, then He would have possessed two complete natures—one human, the other divine. He would have had two centers of consciousness, two minds, two wills. But if the only aspect of human nature that Jesus possessed was a physical body, then He would have had only one center of consciousness, one mind, one will—completely divine. Christians have always objected to this partial humanity view: if Jesus Christ lacked an essential aspect of human nature, it would be wrong to call Him human. Thus, this view denies the full humanity of Jesus.

The *irrelevant humanity view*[5] believes that we cannot know anything more than a few historical facts about the real Jesus Christ. In addition, it holds that the historical Jesus of Nazareth is unimportant for a relationship with God anyway. At the heart of this view is the belief that the four Gospels (and the rest of the New Testament) contain mostly myths about the real Jesus; they are not reliable sources of historical facts. Instead, the Gospels recount the imaginations and hopes of the early disciples. Thus, they are about the Christ of faith—the preexistent Son of God who performed miracles and was raised from the dead—rather than the Jesus of history.

However, according to this view, only the Christ of faith is important for a relationship with God. But the question should be raised: if the Christ of faith is detached from the Jesus of history, how do we know that our relationship with God is true and not just a figment of our (or someone else's) imagination? Thus, this view denies the relevancy of the humanity of Jesus.

PAUSE TIME

From what you've learned in this chapter, what difference does it make—or should it make—to you that Jesus is a real and fully human being? Reflect especially on the help that He can provide when you face trials and temptations and the model He can be for overcoming temptations and doing what is right in the midst of trouble and suffering.

Does the fact that Jesus never once sinned indicate something to you about God's goal for your life? How do you deal with sin and failure in your life, and what encouragement does 1 John 1:9 bring to you? How does the full range of human activities and emotions exhibited by Jesus—close friendships, love, compassion for strangers, anger and indignation in the face of suffering and need, joy, resolute pursuit of His purpose, wrestling with God's will, the learning of obedience through suffering—help you to better grasp God's purposes for you?

CHAPTER FOUR

IMMANUEL—GOD WITH US

When it comes to Jesus, everyone has an opinion—and often these are quite extreme. Earlier I told you about my talk with Mark. He denied that Jesus is fully God. I also told you about my conversations with Roman Catholics. Many of them struggle with understanding that Jesus is a real man, so they end up denying the fully humanity of Jesus.

Several years ago, a book came out with the title *The Myth of God Incarnate.*[6] One of the opinions in this book is quite extreme in another manner: To say that Jesus Christ is both fully God and fully man is as absurd as saying that this diagram is a circle:

Thus, conflicting views about Jesus challenge us. Some say, "Jesus is not fully God." According to others, "Jesus is not fully human." Still others consider the belief that Jesus is the God-man to be a sure indication that we believers are not fully sane!

How do we as followers of Jesus respond to these extreme opinions?

Seeing Jesus as the God-Man

So far I have presented two key truths: Jesus Christ is fully God, and He is fully human. The next step is for us to consider how Jesus Christ can be both fully divine and fully human at the same time. This is particularly perplexing because His divine attributes—His omniscience (He knows everything), eternity (He has no beginning or end), omnipresence (He is everywhere present), omnipotence (He is all-powerful), and immutability (He never changes)—are the polar opposites of His human attributes—He increased in knowledge; He was born in Bethlehem and lived all of His life around Israel; He needed nourishment and rest; and He matured physically, socially, intellectually, and spiritually. Despite the mind-blowing nature of this issue, the Bible insists that this is the reality of Jesus Christ—He is fully God and fully man.

This reality is also of critical importance for our salvation. For Jesus Christ to die and pay the penalty for the sins of all people—sins against an infinitely holy God—He had to be fully God. Nothing short of total divinity would suffice. Furthermore, for His death to work on behalf of human beings, He had to be fully human. Nothing short of complete humanity would do. We need the work of the God-man, Jesus Christ, if we hope to experience a salvation that overcomes our sin and reunites us in a personal relationship with God Himself.

Do you grasp how important this is?

The problem was highlighted very early on in the church's history in an interesting description of Jesus Christ:

> Though the Son was incorporeal (without a body), He formed for Himself a body like ours. He appeared as one of the sheep; yet He still remained the shepherd. He was esteemed a servant; yet He did not renounce the Sonship. He was carried in the womb of Mary, yet He was clothed in the nature of His Father. He walked upon the earth; yet He filled heaven. He appeared as an infant; yet He did not discard the eternity of His nature. He was invested with a body, but it did not limit His divinity. He was regarded as poor; yet He was not divested of His riches. He needed food because He was man; yet He did not cease to feed the entire world because He is God. He put on the likeness of a servant, while not impairing the likeness of His Father.[7]

Notice the contrasts presented here:

Jesus

as human being	*as Son of God*
with a body	without a body
a sheep	the shepherd
a servant	the Son
human nature	divine nature
located on earth	filled everywhere
born	always existed
limited	unlimited
regarded as poor	rich beyond measure
ate food	fed the whole world

According to His human nature, Jesus Christ is one thing; according to His divine nature, He is the complete opposite.

As difficult as this might be to understand and accept, the Bible affirms both the divine and human natures of Jesus Christ (Phil. 2:5–8): "Make your own attitude that of Christ Jesus, who, existing in the form of God, did not consider equality with God as something to be used for His own advantage. Instead He emptied Himself by assuming the form of a slave, taking on the likeness of men. And when He had come as a man in His external form, He humbled Himself by becoming obedient to the point of death—even to death on a cross."

Again, note the contrasts:

form of God $\diagdown$ $\diagup$ equality with God
humility unto death $\diagup$ $\diagdown$ form of a human servant

Exalted from all eternity, sharing in the glorious splendor of divine majesty, the Son of God humbled Himself by leaving His place of preeminence and taking on human nature. As the God-man, the divine servant, He obediently faced crucifixion to rescue us from sin and death. While remaining what He always was—God—He became what He had never been—a human being—to accomplish salvation for us.

"Although the word does not explicitly occur in Scripture, the church has used the term *incarnation* to refer to the fact that Jesus was God in human flesh. The *incarnation* was the act of God the Son whereby He took to Himself a human nature."[8] This is also referred to as the *hypostatic union*. *Hypostasis* means *person*; thus, the hypostatic union is *the union of the two natures*—the divine nature and the human nature—*in the one person*, Jesus Christ.

In AD 451, the church expressed this belief in the *Chalcedonian Creed:*

> Following the holy fathers, we all with one accord teach people to acknowledge one and the same Son, our Lord Jesus Christ. He is at once complete in divinity and complete in humanity, truly God and truly man, consisting also of a human soul and body. He is of one nature with the Father as regards His divinity, and at the same time of one nature with us as regards His humanity. He is like us in all respects, apart from sin. As regards His divinity, He was begotten of the Father before the ages, but yet as regards His humanity He was born, for us and for our salvation, of the Virgin Mary, *theotokos* (the God-bearer). He is one and the same Christ, Son, Lord, only-begotten, recognized in two natures—without confusion, without change, without division, without separation. The distinction of the natures was in no way annulled by the union, but rather the characteristics of each nature were preserved. They come together in one person and existence, not as parted or separated into two persons, but one and the same Son and only-begotten God the Word, Lord Jesus Christ.[9]

Clearly, the *Chalcedonian Creed* embraced the belief that Jesus Christ consists of two natures in one person. Also, as we will now see, the creed explicitly denied several errors in thinking and teaching about the God-man.

The Incarnation of Jesus: Errors to Avoid

One error that we have already discussed is *Arianism* and its denial of the full deity of the Son. The *Chalcedonian Creed* specifically affirmed that Jesus Christ is "complete in divinity" and of the same nature as the Father with respect to His deity. We believe that Jesus Christ is fully God.

Another error (again, previously mentioned) is the *partial humanity view*. This view believes that Jesus took on genuine human nature, but not a complete human nature. He possessed a real human body but lacked a human soul. The creed specifically affirmed that Jesus Christ is "complete in humanity . . . truly man, consisting of a human soul and body." He is of the same nature as us with respect to His humanity, except when it comes to sin. We believe that Jesus Christ is fully human.

The *cooperative persons view*[10] believes that two distinct and independent persons worked in conjunction with each other in Jesus Christ. As this view sees it, a divine person—the Son of God—cooperated with a human person—Jesus of Nazareth. But there was no true union of two natures; just cooperation between two persons. The creed explicitly stated that in the incarnation, two natures "come together in one person and existence, not as parted or separated into two persons." We believe that Jesus Christ is one person with two natures.

The *hybrid nature view*[11] believes that when the divine nature and human nature came together in Jesus Christ, the two fused to change into a third kind of nature—a **divine**human or **human**divine nature. (Proponents of this view generally emphasize Jesus' divine nature.) Thus, the divine nature became something other than distinctly divine, and the human nature became something other than distinctly human. The creed specifically stated that Jesus Christ is to be "recognized in two natures, without confusion and without change." His divine nature was preserved as fully divine, and His human nature was preserved as fully human. We believe that Jesus Christ is one person with two natures, and these natures remain distinctly divine and distinctly human. He is the God-man.

Kenoticism (from a Greek word that means *to empty*) believes that during His incarnation, the Son of God willing emptied Himself of His divine attributes. This view takes its idea from Philippians 2:5-8 (cited above) and its emphasis that Jesus Christ "did not consider equality with God as something to be used for His own advantage. Instead, He emptied Himself by assuming the form of a slave." Thus, before the incarnation, Jesus Christ was fully God, but during the incarnation, He purposefully set aside His divine attributes—like omniscience, omnipresence, and omnipotence—so as to become fully human. The problem with this view is that this passage doesn't teach that Jesus Christ emptied Himself of His deity.

Rather, He set aside the glorious splendor of His divine majesty; the Son of God humbled Himself by leaving His preeminent status to become a man. Human nature was *added to* the Son of God; divine nature was *not subtracted from* Him. Besides, how could the Son of God ever empty Himself of His divine nature? Again, we believe that Jesus Christ is the God-man, and He did not sacrifice His deity in becoming incarnate as a human being.

PAUSE TIME

The *Athanasian Creed*, another statement of faith written by the early church, echoes what I have been saying:

> It is necessary for eternal salvation that a person believes correctly the incarnation of our Lord Jesus Christ. This is the correct belief: We believe and affirm that our Lord Jesus Christ, the Son of God, is God and man: God—of the nature of the Father, begotten before the worlds; and man—of the nature of His mother, born into the world. Perfect God and perfect man, being of a human soul and human body. Equal to the Father as regards His divinity, and inferior to the Father as regards His humanity. Although He is God and man, He is not two, but one Christ. One—not by change of the divinity into humanity, but by the assumption of humanity into God. One altogether—not by confusion of natures, but by unity of person.[12]

Do you grasp why "it is necessary for eternal salvation that a person believes correctly the incarnation of our Lord Jesus Christ"? Consider what it would mean for your salvation if Jesus Christ were not fully God. Then consider what it would mean for your salvation if Jesus Christ were not fully human. How could He have paid the infinite penalty for your sins if He were not fully God? How could He have even died for your sins if He were not fully human? Apart from being the God-man, Jesus Christ could not be your Savior.

One more thing: Jesus Christ, as God who became man, set an example for us to follow. Now, clearly, we cannot be God who becomes human, and we can't be human beings who become God! But the example He set for us involves the attitude at the heart of the Son of God becoming human. Such an act—leaving the glorious splendor and majesty of heaven to live among us sinful human beings as one of us—required humility to the point of absolute self-sacrifice. He did not regard His equal status with God the Father to be something that He would selfishly hang on to. So Jesus gave it all up for our sake! And as we read in Philippians 2:5-8, we are to have this same attitude in ourselves. We are to humble and sacrifice ourselves—our reputations, privileges, rights—for the sake of others. Can you think of someone for whom you can sacrifice yourself—some of your time, help, attention, and joy? What specifically and practically can you do in this step of humbling yourself so as to be like Jesus Christ?

CHAPTER FIVE

WDJD?

Several years ago, many Christians wore a bracelet with four letters and a question mark imprinted on it: WWJD? This expression stood for a question that Christians purposed to ask themselves: What Would Jesus Do? The idea was that if a Christian would ask himself what Jesus would do in a situation, then a good idea of what God would want His people to do or think or say in any given situation would become clear.

As you can imagine, this practice gave rise to completely ridiculous notions of God's will. For example, a group of environmentalists maintained that Jesus would drive a fuel-efficient automobile rather than a gas-guzzling SUV. Of course, environmentally sensitive friends of mine countered that Jesus would never even own a car but would take public transportation instead! Can you see how silly the WWJD? mind-set could become?

On the other hand, the idea of asking WWJD? is not wrong in itself; indeed, raising the question can be quite helpful at times. In fact, the Bible encourages this type of thinking: Jesus calls us to imitate Him (Eph. 5:1). Furthermore, "the one who says he remains in Him should walk just as He walked" (1 John 2:6). And Christians throughout the centuries have sought to conform their lives—their actions, thoughts, and words—to the example set by Christ.

So when needing to choose between keeping your commitment to attend the youth group retreat and going to a family reunion scheduled for that same weekend, it could be helpful to ask what Jesus would do. Or when faced with the option of keeping a friend's secret or telling that friend's parents because you fear your friend's actions may harm her, ask yourself what Jesus would do in a similar situation.

Stumped about what Jesus would do in these two scenarios? Asking WWJD? doesn't make our life easy. Both examples point out something crucial: Before we can ask what Jesus would do, we need to ask (and answer) another question: WDJD?—What Did Jesus Do? To help us discern the answer to this question, let's explore the life, relationships, and ministry of Jesus, so we can give an intelligent answer to the bracelet's question.

What Did Jesus Do?

When we think carefully about Jesus Christ as the God-man, we can imagine that His life and ministry were quite complex. As we have noted already, Jesus gave very clear demonstrations of His identity as God, especially through the miracles He performed. Also, Jesus lived as a true and fully human being—sleeping, eating, drinking, building friendships, maturing, and so forth. To say the least, His reality as the God-man meant that Jesus Christ was one who could not be easily figured out.

Beyond this complexity of living as fully God and fully man, Jesus' life and ministry were also paradoxical. On the one hand, He pursued many people—especially those who were marginalized in His culture (those who failed to meet the standards of worth erected by the privileged people)—with unconditional love and acceptance. On the other hand, He rejected many others—especially those who were self-inflated, proud, and boastful and those who failed to understand that "those who are well don't need a doctor, but the sick do" (Matt. 9:12).

Positively, He extended compassion and mercy to the blind, deaf, mute, crippled, and sick by healing many. Negatively, He expressed disappointment in and contempt for the hard-hearted religious leaders of His day.

At times, the divine wisdom that overflowed in His teaching so confounded His listeners that they considered Him a fool—or a demon in disguise. At other times, Jesus' (apparently) foolish counsel—"whoever seeks to keep his life will lose it, and whoever loses his life will preserve it" (Luke 17:33 NASB); "whoever wishes to become great among you shall be your servant" (Matt. 20:26

NASB)—was so countercultural that it is only by faith that we can embrace it and say, "God's foolishness is wiser than human wisdom" (1 Cor. 1:25).

This complex and paradoxical nature of Jesus Christ underscores two important points. First, we must at all costs avoid reducing Jesus by focusing on some aspects of His life and ministry while neglecting other aspects. He is not easily fenced in and restricted according to our own measurements. We must not attempt to limit His many-faceted reality. Second, we must never force Jesus into our own mold, attempting to domesticate Him by reconfiguring Jesus into our own image.[13] Such a portrait of Him would only say a great deal about us and very little about Jesus.

Keeping these points in mind, I will construct a brief summary of Jesus' life and ministry so that we can answer the question, What did Jesus do?

And the challenge will be to let Jesus be Jesus.

Jesus' Teachings

During His three years of ministry, Jesus encountered many people who were hungry for a word from God. Unlike the teaching of His contemporaries—the religious leaders, lawyers, and the scribes—the teaching of Jesus resonated in their hearts and satisfied their craving, as evidenced in Mark 1:21-22: "Then they went into Capernaum, and right away He entered the synagogue on the Sabbath and began to teach. They were astonished at His teaching because, unlike the scribes, He was teaching them as one having authority."

Astonished listeners would commonly wonder, "'Where did this man get these things?' they said. 'What is this wisdom given to Him . . . ?'" (Mark 6:2). Their amazement stemmed in part from the fact that they knew Him as one of their own: "They were all speaking well of Him and were amazed by the gracious words that came from His mouth, yet they said, 'Isn't this Joseph's son?'" (Luke 4:22). They also did not understand how Jesus, who had not gone to school, could teach so well: "Then the Jews were amazed and said, 'How does He know the Scriptures, since He hasn't been trained?'" (John 7:15). The crowds did not expect this kind of teaching from Jesus because, as far as they knew, He was just an ordinary man.

But Jesus' teaching did not come from Himself: "My teaching isn't Mine but is from the One who sent Me. If anyone wants to do His will, he will understand whether the teaching is from God or if I am speaking on My own" (John 7:16–17). Jesus taught what the Father had taught Him. Moreover, Jesus upheld the authority of the Bible of His day—"the Law and the Prophets"; what we Christians now call the Old Testament—and taught people how to understand and obey it rightly: "Don't assume that I came to destroy the Law or the Prophets. I did not come to destroy but to fulfill. For I assure you: Until heaven and earth pass away, not the smallest letter or one stroke of a letter will pass from the law until all things are accomplished. Therefore, whoever breaks one of the least of these commandments and teaches people to do so will be called least in the kingdom of heaven. But whoever practices and teaches [these commandments] will be called great in the kingdom of heaven" (Matt. 5:17–19).

Constantly, Jesus referred His listeners to what was written in the Word of God. This stood in contrast with many of the religious leaders of His day, who either added to the Word through their human traditions or neglected parts of it. But Jesus' attitude toward the Bible was clearly focused: "the Scripture cannot be broken" (John 10:35).

What was it that Jesus taught that drew such astonishment? On the one hand, Jesus' teachings pushed the envelope in terms of what people were accustomed to hearing. For example, He made this contrast: "You have heard that it was said . . . but I tell you . . ." (Matt. 5:21–48), addressing

- murder, explaining that even anger with one's brother brings guilt before God
- fornication, pointing out that even lust in one's heart qualifies as adultery
- divorce, restricting what had become common practice
- vow-swearing, encouraging instead a straightforward "yes" or "no"
- revenge, urging nonresistance against personal attacks
- hatred of enemies, urging love of enemies

These countercultural values were also encouraged in Jesus' Beatitudes. The Beatitudes note that, whereas the world honors people who are wealthy, famous, strong, and successful, God blesses the poor in spirit, those who mourn, the gentle, those who pursue righteousness, the merciful, the pure in heart, the peacemakers, and those who are persecuted (Matt. 5:3-12).

Instead of being consumed by external matters, Jesus urged His followers to focus on matters of the heart (Mark 7:14-23). This meant particularly that when giving money to the poor, praying publicly, and engaging in fasting, His followers should do so in ways that do not draw attention to themselves (Matt. 6:1-21): "Be careful not to practice your righteousness in front of people, to be seen by them. Otherwise, you will have no reward from your Father in heaven" (v. 1).

In place of anxious worrying about the essentials of life—food, drink, clothing, shelter—Jesus challenged His followers to trust in God for their provisions. He noted that if God cares and provides all the essentials of life for birds and flowers—which are here today and gone tomorrow—then how much more will God take care of His followers. So "seek first the kingdom of God and His righteousness, and all these things will be provided for you" (Matt. 6:33).

PAUSE TIME

Doesn't Jesus' teaching on these countercultural values intrigue you? For more, do a study of Matthew 5-7. See if you can list all the contrasts that Jesus urges us to embrace. Then select one or two on which He wants you to work to develop His countercultural values in your life.

On the other hand, Jesus contradicted what people were accustomed to being taught. He strongly renounced the people's reliance upon their own human traditions that weakened or destroyed the Word of God. Jesus said to them:

"You completely invalidate God's command in order to maintain your tradition! For Moses said: 'Honor your father and your mother'; and, 'Whoever speaks evil of father or mother must be put to death.' But you say, 'If a man tells his father or mother: Whatever benefit you might have received from me is Corban'" (that is, a gift committed to the temple), "you no longer let him do

anything for his father or mother. You revoke God's
word by your tradition that you have handed down. And
you do many other similar things." (Mark 7:9–13)

Jesus also contradicted the tradition of highly respecting people
who gave lots of money to the poor: "Sitting across from the
temple treasury, He watched how the crowd dropped money into
the treasury. Many rich people were putting in large sums. And a
poor widow came and dropped in two tiny coins worth very little.
Summoning His disciples, He said to them, 'I assure you: This poor
widow has put in more than all those giving to the temple treasury.
For they all gave out of their surplus, but she out of her poverty
has put in everything she possessed—all she had to live on'" (Mark
12:41–44).

He also dispelled the notion that people who suffer terrible
tragedy in this life must have sinned terribly, mentioning that the
eighteen people who had been crushed by a falling tower in Siloam
(a calamity His listeners would have known about) were no worse
sinners than the inhabitants of Jerusalem. Jesus warned those who
have escaped such suffering to turn back to God or face even worse
eternal tragedy (Luke 13:1–5).

To dispel the belief that self-righteousness makes one favorable to God, Jesus told a parable about a Pharisee (a very religious
person) and a tax collector (a person who profited illegally by col-
lecting taxes):

The Pharisee stood and was praying this to himself:
"God, I thank You that I am not like other people: swin-
dlers, unjust, adulterers, or even like this tax collector.
I fast twice a week; I pay tithes of all that I get." But the
tax collector, standing some distance away, was even
unwilling to lift up his eyes to heaven, but was beating
his breast, saying, "God, be merciful to me, the sinner!"
I tell you, this man went to his house justified [forgiven
by God] rather than the other; for everyone who exalts
himself will be humbled, but he who humbles himself
will be exalted. (Luke 18:11–14 NASB)

Jesus also confounded those who denied that righteous people will
be resurrected from the dead: "But that the dead are raised, even
Moses showed, in the passage about the burning bush, where he

calls the Lord 'The God of Abraham, and the God of Isaac, and the God of Jacob.' Now He is not the God of the dead, but of the living; for all live to Him" (Luke 20:37–38 NASB).

The only response possible to Jesus was to compliment His teaching. "For they did not have courage to question Him any longer about anything" (Luke 20:40 NASB).

PAUSE TIME

Jesus corrected wrong thoughts, attitudes, and beliefs. His listeners had a wrong emphasis on tradition ("We've always done it this way!") over God's Word. They had a wrong respect for the rich over the poor. They held a wrong idea about why some people suffer. They believed a wrong notion of how to obtain God's favor and about the resurrection. These corrections are not very popular in our world today, but why do you think they are so important? Are there any places in your life that Jesus is correcting? What should your response to His correction be?

The story of the Pharisee and tax collector was just one of many parables with which Jesus regularly taught the people of His day. A *parable* teaches an important spiritual truth (that is unfamiliar to its audience) by means of analogy with something concrete (that is familiar to its audience). Many of Jesus' analogies used either metaphors (for example, calling someone who communicates the gospel a "sower") or similes ("the kingdom of God is like . . ."). Certain elements of the parables, but not all of them, are symbolic, representing someone or something else.[14] On most occasions, the disciples needed Jesus to explain His parables for them to understand His meaning.

Jesus often taught about the kingdom of God using parables. Some key analogies that Jesus used include the following:

the kingdom of God is like . . .	the analogy means the kingdom . . .
various kinds of soils	will encounter different types of reactions
wheat and weeds	will achieve success amid opposition
a mustard seed	starts very small yet will grow very large

yeast	will permeate throughout everything
hidden treasure/a costly pearl	is worth giving up everything to obtain
a net to catch fish	will lead to the separation of the righteous and the wicked
a king settling accounts	requires those who are forgiven to forgive
a landowner paying wages	goes beyond fairness to include grace
two sons	is embraced by sinners rather than righteous people
a wedding banquet	is treated badly by the Jewish people
ten virgins	requires preparedness because of its delay
talents of money	demands growth of its subjects' resources
the separation of sheep and goats	anticipates the separation of the righteous and wicked based on treatment of the disciples
a seed that sprouts and grows	develops supernaturally

Jesus used parables to teach other important spiritual truths. The debts of two men—one owed fifty denarii (a denarius was about one day's pay), the other owed five hundred denarii (ten times as much as the other)—were forgiven. Jesus used this parable to emphasize that the person who is forgiven much, loves much; but the person who is forgiven little, loves little (Luke 7:41–43).

In response to a lawyer's question about who is his neighbor, Jesus offered the story of the good Samaritan. This parable reversed the lawyer's focus: rather than wondering who your neighbor is, you should be concerned about being a good neighbor to others (Luke 10:25–37). The parable of a rich fool, who concentrated all his efforts on acquiring and maintaining wealth for the sake of his own ease and comfort, becomes a shocking rebuke of those who are not rich toward God (Luke 12:13–21).

In a series of three parables about lostness—a man has lost one of his sheep, a woman has lost one of her coins, a father has lost one of his sons—Jesus teaches about the joy that is experienced when that which was lost is found (Luke 15).

The parable of the rich man and Lazarus (not the Lazarus who was brother to Mary and Martha and was raised from the dead) teaches that in the life to come, one's fortunes will be reversed: The rich man, who enjoyed all the comforts of this life and ignored the treasures of the afterlife, experiences loss and great torment in eternity, whereas the poor man, who knew nothing but pain and tragedy in this life, experiences comfort in the life to come (Luke 16:19–31).

Today, we echo the question the disciples posed to Jesus: "Why do You speak to [the people] in parables?" (Matt. 13:10). He offered two reasons for this teaching method. The first reason had to do with the favored position of the disciples in Jesus' kingdom mission, as He explained to them: "To you it has been granted to know the mysteries of the kingdom of heaven, but to them [the crowds] it has not been granted" (Matt. 13:11 NASB). This reason underscores why Jesus often explained His parables to His disciples: He wanted to ensure that they understood His meaning and grasped important truth about the kingdom He was building and which they would be leading.

The second reason focused on God's sovereign choice that the crowds who hung around Jesus would not be permitted to comprehend His teaching: "Therefore I speak to them in parables; because while seeing they do not see, and while hearing they do not hear, nor do they understand" (Matt. 13:13 NASB). As difficult as this might be for us to grasp, the fact remains that God did not will for the crowds watching and listening to Jesus to "see" and "hear" (that is, "understand") Him. Indeed, this was God's design from centuries past. Specifically, Isaiah the prophet had predicted this (Isa. 6:9–10) nearly eight hundred years before Jesus taught in parables.

> In their case the prophecy of Isaiah is being fulfilled,
> which says,
>> "You will keep on hearing, but will not understand;
>> you will keep on seeing, but will not perceive;
>> for the heart of this people has become dull,
>> with their ears they scarcely hear,
>> and they have closed their eyes,
>> otherwise they would see with their eyes,
>> hear with their ears,

and understand with their heart and return,
and I would heal them." (Matt. 13:14–15 NASB)

So Jesus taught the crowds in parables, partially hiding the truth He was communicating. This was both by divine design— God would not grant understanding to the crowds following Jesus—and due to the dullness of those same followers—they had failed to carry out their human responsibility to pay attention to and learn from Jesus.

The crowds who watched and listened to Him expected the kingdom of God to come with great power to destroy their enemies and reward them with prosperity and security. Jesus veiled the truth in parables to emphasize something completely unexpected: The kingdom of God would not only come with great power in the future; it was also present and active in the person and work of Jesus Christ. This advance intervention of the kingdom was only for the disciples to grasp because they would continue the work of their Master once He was gone.

PAUSE TIME

Aren't the parables of Jesus strange? On the one hand, like good mysteries, they are fun and interesting to figure out. On the other hand, they are often hard to figure out. Does your status as a follower of Jesus and His desire for you to under-stand these parables give you hope to figure them out? Try reading some of the parables and search for clues in them to help you understand what Jesus is teaching.

Jesus' Discipling

While Jesus clearly spent a great amount of His time teaching large crowds of people, He focused a significant part of His efforts on a small group of men. Known as the disciples or apostles, these closest followers of Jesus were taught and prepared by Him to take over His work after His death and resurrection. Most of them were personally challenged by Jesus to leave everything they had to dedicate themselves to following Him, as these brothers did:

As He was walking along the Sea of Galilee, He saw
two brothers, Simon, who was called Peter, and his

brother Andrew. They were casting a net into the sea, since they were fishermen. "Follow Me," He told them, "and I will make you fishers of men!" Immediately they left their nets and followed Him. Going on from there, He saw two other brothers, James the son of Zebedee, and his brother John. They were in a boat with Zebedee their father, mending their nets, and He called them. Immediately they left the boat and their father and followed Him. (Matt 4:18–22)

Jesus' choice disciples sometimes plunged Him into trouble with the religious leaders who opposed Him:

Jesus went out and saw a tax collector named Levi sitting at the tax office, and He said to him, "Follow Me!" So, leaving everything behind, he got up and began to follow Him. Then Levi hosted a grand banquet for Him at his house. Now there was a large crowd of tax collectors and others who were guests with them. But the Pharisees and their scribes were complaining to His disciples, "Why do you eat and drink with tax collectors and sinners?" Jesus replied to them, "The healthy don't need a doctor, but the sick do. I have not come to call the righteous, but sinners to repentance." (Luke 5:27–32)

The group of disciples whom Jesus called was small, but they were appointed to carry out a profoundly important purpose: Jesus "went up the mountain and summoned those He wanted, and they came to Him. He also appointed twelve—He also named them apostles—to be with Him, to send them out to preach, and to have authority to drive out demons" (Mark 3:13–15).

The twelve disciples embarked on their ministry of preaching about the kingdom of God and healing the sick, raising the dead, cleansing the lepers, and casting out demons (Matt. 10:7–8). They were not to bring extra food, clothes, and other supplies with them; instead, they were to entrust themselves completely to God and His ability to supply all their needs (Matt. 10:9–15). Jesus promised them fierce persecution and bitter contempt for their missionary efforts: "Brother will betray brother to death, and a father his child. Children will even rise up against their parents and have them put to death. You will be hated by everyone because of My name. But the one who endures to the end will be delivered" (Matt. 10:21–22).

Indeed, Jesus challenged all who considered following Him to count the cost of discipleship: "If anyone comes to Me and does not hate his own father and mother, wife and children, brothers and sisters—yes, and even his own life—he cannot be My disciple. Whoever does not bear his own cross and come after Me cannot be My disciple. For which of you, wanting to build a tower, doesn't first sit down and calculate the cost to see if he has enough to complete it? Otherwise, after he has laid the foundation and cannot finish it, all the onlookers will begin to make fun of him" (Luke 14:26–29).

To those who would be His faithful disciples, however, Jesus offered incredible rewards: "Truly I say to you, there is no one who has left house or brothers or sisters or mother or father or children or farms, for My sake and the gospel's sake, but that he will receive a hundred times as much now in the present age, houses and brothers and sisters and mothers and children and farms, along with persecutions; and in the age to come, eternal life" (Mark 10:29–30 NASB).

With such exacting demands placed on those who would follow Him, it should be no surprise that Jesus' group of disciples was small during His earthly ministry. The twelve apostles were His constant companions, but even one of them—Judas—ultimately ended up betraying Him. On at least one occasion, Jesus expanded His missionary band to include seventy more people, telling them, "The harvest is plentiful, but the laborers are few; therefore beseech the Lord of the harvest to send out laborers into His harvest" (Luke 10:2 NASB).

In addition to these, a significant group of women traveled with the disciples to support their missionary efforts. This group included "some women who had been healed of evil spirits and sicknesses: Mary who was called Magdalene, from whom seven demons had gone out, and Joanna the wife of Chuza, Herod's steward, and Susanna, and many others who were contributing to their support out of their private means" (Luke 8:2–3 NASB).

As the disciples shared progressively in His life and ministry of preaching, healing, and casting out demons, Jesus shared progressively with them the bittersweet destiny of His life and ministry. On at least three occasions, Jesus revealed the tragic and glorious future that awaited Him: "From that time Jesus began to show His disciples that He must go to Jerusalem, and suffer many things from the elders and chief priests and scribes, and be killed, and be raised up on the third day" (Matt. 16:21 NASB; see Matt. 17:22–23 and 20:17–19 for the two other instances).

The disciples' response to this revelation consisted of shock, grief, rebuke, and a naïve fight to claim important roles in Jesus' coming kingdom. But He refused to be distracted by His disciples' misunderstanding of His divinely designed destiny; rather, He "resolutely set out for Jerusalem" (Luke 9:51 NIV) where death by crucifixion awaited Him. Then, when arrested for trial, His disciples abandoned Him. Indeed, Judas betrayed Him by plotting with Jesus' enemies to hand Him over to them, and Peter, His closest disciple, denied that He even knew Jesus.

Even after three years of intense, personal discipleship, the followers of Jesus never grasped the true meaning of His life and ministry. On the contrary, with few exceptions, the disciples demonstrated a consistent misunderstanding of their friend and leader.

Thankfully (as we will see later in the book), the death of Jesus was not the end of Him. Nor was it the end of the disciples and their crucial involvement in establishing the church and expanding the kingdom of God throughout the entire world. Even before He was executed, Jesus gave His disciples a lasting celebration during His final meal with them that would vividly portray His death for the world: "While they were eating, Jesus took some bread, and after a blessing, He broke it and gave it to the disciples, and said, 'Take, eat; this is My body.' And when He had taken a cup and given thanks, He gave it to them, saying, 'Drink from it, all of you; for this is My blood of the covenant, which is poured out for many for forgiveness of sins'" (Matt. 26:26–28 NASB). In this manner, Jesus instituted the *Lord's Supper* (also called *communion* and the *Eucharist*) as a perpetual symbol of His broken body and shed blood for the sins of the world.

At the close of His earthly ministry, Jesus instituted one more lasting celebration for His disciples to observe. This was on the occasion of one of His post-resurrection appearances to His disciples:

"Jesus came up and spoke to them, saying, 'All authority has been given to Me in heaven and on earth. Go therefore and make disciples of all the nations, baptizing them in the name of the Father and the Son and the Holy Spirit, teaching them to observe all that I commanded you; and lo, I am with you always, even to the end of the age'" (Matt. 28:18–20 NASB). In this manner, Jesus instituted baptism as a perpetual symbol of His followers' identification with His death (as we are immersed under the baptismal water) and His resurrection (as we are brought up out of the water).

PAUSE TIME

Imagine what it might have been like to be one of the original disciples of Jesus. Would you have dropped whatever you were doing and followed Him when He called you? Would you have better understood Jesus than the other disciples did? Would you have grasped His mission and been willing to give up everything just to be part of it? Or, like Judas, would you have betrayed Him? Or, like Peter, would you have denied ever knowing Him?

Enough imagination. Let's face your current reality. Certainly, Jesus is calling you to be His disciple. Will you put Him first in all you are and do? Will you give yourself completely to His cause? Will you purpose never to let Him down?

What will it cost you to answer yes to these questions? Will you count the cost and be a disciple of Jesus?

Jesus' Kingdom Mission

Furthering the kingdom of God was the very reason that the Son became incarnate as Jesus Christ and focused much of His life and ministry on His disciples. The very first activity with which Jesus launched His ministry was preaching (He was about thirty years old then): "Repent, for the kingdom of God is at hand" (Matt. 4:17 NASB).

The kingdom is God's reign and rule over all that He created. Jesus' message of repentance was addressed to people who had rejected God's rulership in their lives, forging their own "kingdom" in which they reigned supreme—self-centered, self-righteous, self-loving. Jesus urged His listeners to abdicate their self-rule and to submit themselves to God's gracious and wise rule over them. Indeed, Jesus Himself was the perfect model of what He preached:

He was fully submitted to the Father's will for Him and came to serve. He taught His disciples to do likewise: "You know that those who are recognized as rulers of the Gentiles lord it over them; and their great men exercise authority over them. But it is not this way among you, but whoever wishes to become great among you shall be your servant; and whoever wishes to be first among you shall be slave of all. For even the Son of Man did not come to be served, but to serve, and to give His life a ransom for many" (Mark 10:42–45 NASB).

As servants of all, the disciples were appointed by Jesus to preach the same message about the kingdom of God. This was to be communicated first and foremost to Jesus' own people, the Jews: "Jesus sent out after instructing them [the twelve]: 'Do not go in the way of the Gentiles, and do not enter any city of the Samaritans; but rather go to the lost sheep of the house of Israel. And as you go, preach, saying, "The kingdom of heaven is at hand"'" (Matt. 10:5–7 NASB).

Jesus modeled this emphasis. For example, after pursuing Zaccheus and bringing about his repentance, Jesus noted, "Today salvation has come to this house, because he {Zaccheus], too, is a son of Abraham [that is, Jewish]. For the Son of Man has come to seek and to save that which was lost" (Luke 19:9–10 NASB).

This priority, however, did not mean that others were excluded from the ministry of Jesus and the disciples. A centurion (a non-Jewish Roman soldier), whose servant was suffering paralysis, acknowledged that Jesus had the authority to make the sick man well again. Jesus was astonished: "Truly I say to you, I have not found such great faith with anyone in Israel" (Matt. 8:10 NASB). He was similarly amazed by a Canaanite (non-Jewish) woman who pleaded with Him to rescue her demon-possessed daughter:

> He did not say a word to her. So His disciples approached Him and urged Him, "Send her away because she cries out after us." He replied, "I was sent only to the lost sheep of the house of Israel." But she came, knelt before Him, and said, "Lord, help me!" He answered, "It isn't right to take the children's bread and throw it to their dogs." "Yes, Lord," she said, "yet even the dogs eat the crumbs that fall from their masters' table!" Then

Jesus replied to her, "Woman, your faith is great. Let it
be done for you as you want." And from that moment
her daughter was cured. (Matt. 15:23-28)

On another occasion, Jesus approached a Samaritan woman
(Samaritans were part Jewish and part Gentile, and consequently
disrespected by the Jews). Through His conversation with her, the
Samaritan believed in Jesus. In turn, she testified to her friends
and acquaintances about Him: "From that city [Sychar] many of
the Samaritans believed in Him because of the word of the woman
who testified, 'He told me all the things that I have done.' So when
the Samaritans came to Jesus, they were asking Him to stay with
them; and He stayed there two days. Many more believed because
of His word; and they were saying to the woman, 'It is no longer
because of what you said that we believe, for we have heard for ourselves and know that this One is indeed the Savior of the world'"
(John 4:39-42 NASB).

Clearly, then, Jesus' ministry was not confined to reaching the
Jews with the gospel of the kingdom of God. Indeed, Jesus sadly
expressed that God's focus on the Jewish people would soon come
to end. Speaking to the Jewish religious leaders, Jesus explained: "I
say to you, the kingdom of God will be taken away from you and
given to a people [the non-Jewish people] producing the fruit of it"
(Matt. 21:43 NASB). As the Good Shepherd of all the sheep, Jesus
noted that He came to give His life for both Jews and Gentiles,
thus pleasing the Father: "I lay down my life for the sheep [Jews].
I have other sheep [Gentiles], which are not of this fold; I must
bring them also, and they will hear My voice; and they will become one flock with one shepherd. For this reason the Father loves
Me, because I lay down My life so that I may take it again" (John
10:15-17 NASB).

So while Jesus initially focused His ministry on His own Jewish
people, He anticipated a day in which this concentration would be
extended to people everywhere. This was at the heart of His promise to the disciples, after Peter acknowledged publicly that Jesus was
the Son of God: "I say to you that you are Peter [petros in Greek,
meaning, a stone], and upon this rock [petra, a large rock] I will
build My church; and the gates of Hades [the world of the dead]
will not overpower it" (Matt. 16:18 NASB).

Furthermore, this was at the heart of His commission to His disciples, as He spoke to them before ascending from earth into heaven: "All authority has been given to Me in heaven and on earth. Go therefore and make disciples of all the nations, baptizing them in the name of the Father and the Son and the Holy Spirit, teaching them to observe all that I commanded you; and lo, I am with you always, even to the end of the age" (Matt. 28:18–20 NASB). Through His disciples, who would in turn make more disciples, Jesus' kingdom ministry—calling people to abandon their self-rule and submit to God's reign over them—would be extended to people everywhere throughout all time.

PAUSE TIME

Do you realize that you live in one of the most exciting times in the history of the world? Even as you are reading this, Jesus Christ is fulfilling His promise to build His church. The good news of Jesus Christ and the kingdom of God is expanding into areas that have never before heard it. Have you ever considered joining this missionary force by going on a short-term missions trip with your church? How can you become more involved in helping to fulfill Jesus' Great Commission (Matt. 28:18-20)?

Jesus' Conflicts

But God's reign over people through the expanding kingdom would never come easily. Indeed, Jesus experienced many conflicts as He initiated and developed His kingdom ministry. On one level, He battled temptations and attacks from Satan. Immediately after His baptism, Jesus was led by the Holy Spirit into the wilderness where, after forty days of fasting, He was tempted by the devil. These traps set for Jesus—to turn stones into bread to satisfy His hunger, to attempt to destroy Himself to prove the Father's protection of Him, and to worship Satan so as to gain all the kingdoms of this world—were designed to detour Him from accomplishing God's will. Jesus repulsed each of these satanic temptations by relying on the Word of God (Matt. 4:1–11; Luke 4:1–12).[15]

On another level, Jesus' conflicts were with the people who stood opposed to Him and His mission. Occasionally, these conflicts were with the high-ranking rulers of His day. For example, about two years after Jesus' birth, Herod the Great ordered the killing of "all the male children in and around Bethlehem who were two years old and under" (Matt. 2:16). Herod's infanticide was targeted at killing Jesus, but other children bore the brunt of this conflict. Also, as we will see, Jesus' suffering and death were ultimately approved and carried out by the Roman authorities in Jerusalem.

Jesus' conflicts, however, were primarily with His own people. For example, Jesus provoked an intense reaction when He taught that God's healing and care are not reserved for the Jews: "When they heard this, everyone in the synagogue was enraged. They got up, drove Him out of town, and brought Him to the edge of the hill their town was built on, intending to hurl Him over the cliff. But He passed right through the crowd and went on His way" (Luke 4:28–30).

Even Jesus' miracles occasionally got Him into trouble. For example, Jesus met a Gerasene man who was tortured by a demon: "Many times it had seized him, and although he was guarded, bound by chains and shackles, he would snap the restraints and be driven by the demon into deserted places" (Luke 8:29). After casting out the demon, Jesus sent it into a herd of pigs, which then jumped into a lake and were drowned. But this miracle spooked the townspeople, who asked Jesus to hit the road: "Then people went out to see what had happened. They came to Jesus and found the man the demons had departed from, sitting at Jesus' feet, dressed and in his right mind. And they were afraid. Meanwhile the eyewitnesses reported to them how the demon-possessed man was delivered. Then all the people of the Gerasene region asked Him to leave them, because they were gripped by great fear" (Luke 8:35–37).

Jesus also experienced conflicts with the members of His own family. As previously mentioned, they were convinced that He was mentally disturbed and thought to take Him away and save Him from further embarrassment and risk to His own life. But Jesus refused to relate to His family according to the usual family conventions of His time. Though they tried to take advantage of their blood ties with Him, Jesus would not allow Himself to be controlled by the physical lines of relationship: "He was still speaking to the crowds when suddenly His mother and brothers were standing outside wanting to speak to Him. . . . But He replied to the one who told Him, 'Who is My mother and who are My brothers?' And stretching out His hand toward His disciples, He said, 'Here are My mother and My brothers! For whoever does the will of My Father in heaven, that person is My brother and sister and mother" (Matt. 12:46, 48–50).

These conflicts were particularly fierce when the religious leaders of the Jews were involved. They were upset by the company Jesus kept: "While He was reclining at the table in Levi's house, many tax collectors and sinners were also guests with Jesus and His disciples, because there were many who were following Him. When the scribes of the Pharisees saw that He was eating with sinners and tax collectors, they asked His disciples, 'Why does He eat with tax collectors and sinners?' When Jesus heard this, He told them, 'Those who are well don't need a doctor, but the sick do need one. I didn't come to call the righteous, but sinners'" (Mark 2:15–17). They were also angered by His exorcisms. On one occasion, Jesus cast out a demon from a blind and mute man: "When the Pharisees heard this, they said, 'The man drives out demons only by Beelzebul, the ruler of the demons'" (Matt. 12:24). Jesus responded with a dire warning about committing an unpardonable sin.

Furthermore, the religious leaders were disturbed by His teachings and so confronted Jesus. They were no match for Him, however:

"Tell us, by what authority are You doing these things? Who is it who gave You this authority?" He answered them, "I will also ask you a question. Tell Me, was the baptism of John from heaven or from men?" They discussed it among themselves: "If we say, 'From heaven,' He will say, 'Why didn't you believe him?' But if we say, 'From men,' all the people will stone us, because they are convinced that John was a prophet." So they answered that they did not know its origin. And Jesus said to them, "Neither will I tell you by what authority I do these things." (Luke 20:2–8)

After one occasion in which Jesus told a particularly pointed parable condemning these leaders, "Then the scribes and the chief priests looked for a way to get their hands on Him that very hour, because they knew He had told this parable against them, but they feared the people. They watched closely and sent spies who pretended to be righteous, so they could catch Him in what He said, to hand Him over to the governor's rule and authority" (Luke 20:19-20).

Even more blatantly, Jesus denounced the religious leaders with "Woe to you, scribes and Pharisees, hypocrites!" He addressed them as blind guides, serpents, and a brood of vipers. Jesus specifically condemned them for not practicing what they preached, for putting on a religious show without substance, for seeking the applause of people rather than God, for encumbering the path to heaven with religious rules and regulations, for neglecting the most important matters of life, and so forth (Matt. 23).

In addition to His questionable companions, exorcisms, and teachings, Jesus' persistent claims to enjoy a special relationship with God infuriated His enemies. For instance, Jesus healed a man on the Sabbath, and when the man told the Jews that it was Jesus who had healed him, it sent the Jewish rulers' blood boiling. "Therefore, the Jews began persecuting Jesus because He was doing these things on the Sabbath. But Jesus responded to them, 'My Father is still working, and I am working also.' This is why the Jews began trying all the more to kill Him: not only was He breaking the Sabbath, but He was even calling God His own Father, making Himself equal with God" (John 5:16-18).

After three years of hounding Jesus, the religious leaders finally succeeded in conspiring together to arrest Him after numerous failed attempts. Why then and not earlier, though He'd been vulnerable to being killed (was taken to a cliff to be hurled off by the crowd, according to Luke 4:28-30, and was nearly stoned twice, according to John 8-10) and arrested (was surrounded by temple guards intent on seizing Him, according to John 7:25-47)? Because God was in control of the events of His ministry: "they tried to seize Him. Yet no one laid a hand on Him because His hour had not yet come" (John 7:30). We will further discuss this point and His final arrest in the next chapter.

PAUSE TIME

We've already looked at Jesus' conflicts as clear evidence that He was a real and fully human being. Now let's consider these conflicts as clear indicators of what it might cost us to be His followers. After all, Jesus promised, "If the world hates you, understand that it hated Me before it hated you. If you were of the world, the world would love you as its own. However, because you are not of the world, but I have chosen you out of the world, this is why the world hates you. Remember the word I spoke to you: 'A slave is not greater than his master.' If they persecuted Me, they will also persecute you" (John 15:18-20).

Paul echoed Christ's words: "For it has been given to you on Christ's behalf not only to believe in Him, but also to suffer for Him" (Phil. 1:29). How can Jesus' nearly constant turmoil with conflicts help prepare you for similar struggles you will encounter as His disciple?

Jesus' Relationship with God the Father

Though the conflicts with His enemies were distressing and destructive, Jesus' relationship with His Father was exponentially more comforting and sustaining. We would be hard-pressed to come up with another explanation for Jesus' productive ministry and steady progress in the face of great odds than this Father-Son relationship.

This privileged status was foretold even before Jesus' miraculous conception. The angel announced the miracle to Mary, Jesus' future mother: "Now listen: You will conceive and give birth to a son, and you will call His name JESUS. He will be great and will be called the Son of the Most High" (Luke 1:31-32).

Even at age twelve, Jesus was conscious of a special relationship with God. Remember how His parents and family left Jerusalem to return home after their annual trek to the temple for the Passover, while Jesus remained behind? After a frantic search failed to turn Him up, His parents returned to Jerusalem and found their lost child among the religious teachers, who were amazed by His insights: "And His mother said to Him, 'Son, why have You treated us like this? Your father and I have been anxiously searching for You.' 'Why were you searching for Me?' He asked them. 'Didn't you know that I had to be in my Father's house?' But they did not understand what He said to them" (Luke 2:48-50).

As Jesus' three-year ministry commenced, the Father publicly praised His Son at His baptism: "As soon as He came up out of the water, He saw the heavens being torn open and the Spirit descending to Him like a dove. And a voice came from heaven: 'You are My beloved Son; I take delight in You!'" (Mark 1:10-11).

This love relationship between the Father and the Son meant that the two shared everything together: "The Father loves the Son and has given all things into His hands" (John 3:35). As Jesus Himself prayed: "I praise You, Father, Lord of heaven and earth, because You have hidden these things from the wise and learned and revealed them to infants. Yes, Father, because this was Your good pleasure. All things have been entrusted to Me by My Father. No one knows the Son except the Father, and no one knows the Father except the Son and anyone to whom the Son desires to reveal Him" (Matt. 11:25-27).

This reciprocal loving relationship with the Father was so important for Him that Jesus spoke several times about it shortly before His death. At one point Jesus told the disciples, "[I am going away] so that the world may know that I love the Father. Just as the Father commanded Me, so I do" (John 14:31). A bit later, when praying to the Father for His disciples, Jesus again underscored this love: "Father, I desire those You have given Me to be with Me where I am. Then they will see My glory, which You have given Me because You loved Me before the world's foundation. Righteous Father! The world has not known You. However, I have known You, and these have known that You sent Me. I made Your name known to them and will make it known, so the love You have loved Me with may be in them and I may be in them" (John 17:24-26).

Clearly, the love between the Father and the Son was a primary motivation for Jesus to sacrifice His own life for the world. It was the reason for His constant obedience to the Father's will. Indeed, this relationship accounted for every word He uttered and every action He took:

> I assure you: The Son is not able to do anything on
> His own, but only what He sees the Father doing. For
> whatever the Father does, the Son also does these things
> in the same way. For the Father loves the Son and shows
> Him everything He is doing, and He will show Him
> greater works than these so that you will be amazed. And
> just as the Father raises the dead and gives them life, so
> the Son also gives life to anyone He wants to. The Father,

in fact, judges no one but has given all judgment to the Son, so that all people will honor the Son just as they honor the Father. Anyone who does not honor the Son does not honor the Father who sent Him. (John 5:19–23)

As Jesus obediently followed the kingdom mission mapped out for Him by the Father, He consciously remembered, "I have come down from heaven, not to do My will, but the will of Him who sent Me" (John 6:38). At the end of His ministry, Jesus was able to say to the Father, "I have glorified You on the earth, by completing the work You gave Me to do" (John 17:4).

Accomplishing the Father's work was no easy task. Consider Christ's wretched struggle in the garden of Gethsemane, when He prayed about His impending death (the "cup" being crucifixion on the cross): "'Father, if You are willing, remove this cup from Me; yet not My will, but Yours be done.' Now an angel from heaven appeared to Him, strengthening Him. And being in agony He was praying more fervently; and His sweat became like drops of blood, falling down upon the ground" (Luke 22:42–44 NASB). As He had always done, Jesus continued to willingly choose to do His Father's will when the greatest challenge loomed before Him. "During His earthly life, He offered prayers and appeals, with loud cries and tears, to the One who was able to save Him from death, and He was heard because of His reverence. Though a Son, He learned obedience through what He suffered. After He was perfected, He became the source of eternal salvation to all who obey Him" (Heb. 5:7–9).

His relationship with the Father guided and strengthened Jesus throughout His life and, ultimately, His death for us.

PAUSE TIME

This intimate relationship between the Father and the Son means something absolutely critical for us. While Jesus taught, acted, healed, rebuked, and comforted as God the Father Himself would, this understanding of Jesus isn't comprehensive enough. Jesus revealed the Father, so that when we know Jesus, we know God.

This is so critical because "no one has ever seen God, but God the One and Only, who is at the Father's side, has made him known" (John 1:18 NIV). This was Jesus' very point when one of His disciples approached Him: "Philip said to Him, 'Lord, show us the Father, and it is enough for us.' Jesus said to him, 'Have I been so long with you, and yet you have not come to

know Me, Philip? He who has seen Me has seen the Father'" (John
14:8-9 NASB).
 So what is God like? In one sense, we can never know because the Father has never been seen and cannot be seen. In
another awesome sense, however, we can know God because Jesus
reveals Him to us. So focus on Jesus and you will know God:
"And Jesus cried out and said, 'He who believes in Me, does not
believe in Me but in Him who sent Me. He who sees Me sees the
One who sent Me. I have come as Light into the world, so that
everyone who believes in Me will not remain in darkness'" (John
12:44-46 NASB).
 Can you help any of your friends to see this light so they
may know God revealed in Jesus?

Jesus' Relationship with God the Holy Spirit

In addition to His bond with the Father, Jesus also enjoyed a
relationship with the Holy Spirit. Jesus' existence as the incarnate
Son of God was made possible by the Holy Spirit, as the angel explained to Mary about her upcoming pregnancy: "The Holy Spirit
will come upon you, and the power of the Most High will over-
shadow you; and for that reason the holy Child shall be called the
Son of God" (Luke 1:35 NASB). And when Joseph doubted the le-
gitimacy of Mary's pregnancy and planned to separate from her,
he was told, "Joseph, son of David, do not be afraid to take Mary
as your wife; for the Child who has been conceived in her is of the
Holy Spirit" (Matt. 1:20 NASB).

The next time we see the Spirit active with Jesus is at His baptism, when "the Holy Spirit descended upon Him in bodily form
like a dove" (Luke 3:22 NASB). Clearly, the Spirit miraculously and
personally prepared Jesus for His kingdom mission.

Throughout His earthly ministry, Jesus was guided by the Spirit.
In a surprising development, "Jesus, full of the Holy Spirit, returned
from the Jordan and was led around by the Spirit in the wilderness"
(Luke 4:1 NASB). It was in the wilderness that Jesus came face-to-
face with the devil, experiencing intense temptations. And it was
the Spirit who propelled Jesus to confront His archenemy! The victory achieved over the tempter in this situation readied Jesus for the
tougher struggles He was to face over the next three years.

As Jesus began His ministry, He appeared in the Nazareth synagogue and read from the prophecy of Isaiah:

The Spirit of the Lord is upon Me,

Because He anointed Me to preach the gospel to the poor.

He has sent Me to proclaim release to the captives,

And recovery of sight to the blind,

To set free those who are oppressed,

To proclaim the favorable year of the Lord.

(Isaiah 61:1-2; Luke 4:18-19 NASB)

Clearly, Jesus was conscious of carrying out His ministry with the presence and power of the Holy Spirit.

This empowerment was especially evident in Jesus' exorcisms. Jesus cast out demons by means of the Holy Spirit. Now His enemies claimed that Jesus actually exorcised evil spirits by Beelzebub, the leader of the demons. Jesus, however, pointed out how absurd their reasoning was: "Any kingdom divided against itself is laid waste; and any city or house divided against itself will not stand. If Satan casts out Satan, he is divided against himself; how then will his kingdom stand? If I by Beelzebub cast out demons, by whom do your sons cast them out? For this reason they will be your judges. But if I cast out demons by the Spirit of God, then the kingdom of God has come upon you" (Matt. 12:25-28 NASB).

Despite His enemies' claims to the contrary, Jesus engaged in His ministry of exorcising demons through the power of the Holy Spirit.

Through His teaching, discipling, temptations, conflicts, and whatever else He did, Jesus walked "in the power of the Spirit" (Luke 4:14). So intense was this relationship between the Son and the Spirit that John the Baptist underscored it: "For God sent Him [the Son], and He speaks God's words, since He gives the Spirit without measure" (John 3:34). There was no end to the Spirit's presence in Jesus, no interruption of the Spirit's empowerment of Jesus, no partial expression of the Spirit's work through Jesus. As the God-man, Jesus was completely and consistently guided by the Holy Spirit.

PAUSE TIME

Do you see how Jesus' relationship with the Holy Spirit is the perfect model for us as we seek to please God and carry out His will? The apostle Paul commands, "And don't get drunk with wine, which [leads to] reckless actions, but be filled with the Spirit" (Eph. 5:18). We are not to allow anything—specifically wine, and by extension drugs, popularity, sex, athletic acclaim, academic recognition, work, etc.—to so dominate our lives that we engage in excesses that go against the will of God. Rather, we are to yield the control of our lives to the Holy Spirit. It is He who should be the dominating person, the focus of our constant attention, so that all that we are and do pleases God.

Consider Jesus' model of being filled with the Holy Spirit. Will you purpose to obey the command to be filled with the Spirit? Begin each day by acknowledging the Spirit's control of your life, then throughout the day, ask Him to guide and direct you. By doing so, you will follow the example of Jesus!

And so Jesus engaged in teaching, discipling, facing conflicts, furthering the kingdom of God, and relating to both the Father and the Holy Spirit. Now that we can answer the question, WDJD? we are in a far better position to ask ourselves WWJD? the next time we are faced with a critical choice or need guidance in a decision we should make. The more familiar we become with what Jesus did, the more authentically and truthfully we will be able to consider what He would do.

PAUSE TIME

Are you facing a particular situation for which you may find help by asking and answering WWJD? Carefully review the appropriate section(s) of this chapter and consider what Jesus did. Then apply that answer to your current situation. And may you have the courage and strength of character to do what Jesus would do.

CHAPTER SIX

DEATH FASHIONED ON A CROSS

Not long after I became a Christian (I was a senior in high school), I began to accumulate crosses. I wore one around my neck, had one engraved on my Bible cover, stuck a cross pin on my shirt, and even signed letters with a cross after my name. When my friends and I met for Bible study and prayer, we sat in a circle on the floor with lighted candles and a wooden cross in our midst. I'm sure that if I were in high school today and embraced Jesus Christ, I would wear a cross earring, a cross ring, and have a cross tattooed on my arm or back or ankle. The cross marked me out as a Christian, as a follower of Jesus Christ, and I was proud to publicly display my allegiance to Him.

Then one day I picked up a book by Francis Schaeffer. Titled *The Mark of the Christian*,[16] it challenged me to consider this question: Do the external signs we display to communicate our commitment to Jesus genuinely mark us out as Christians? Schaeffer concluded that it's not the crosses worn around our necks or dangling from our ears that truly signify that we are followers of Christ. Rather, love is the authentic mark of a Christian.

I've never looked at a cross the same way.

Now today, many people are decorated with crosses; athletes, musicians, actors and actresses, political leaders, and gang members alike wear them. While I look at their crosses and hope that these symbolize a commitment to Christ, I doubt if my expectations are realistic in most cases. More often than not, cross-wearers do not love Jesus and others. Rather, the crosses affixed to rings or etched into their skin are nothing more than stylish decoration.

The cross has become a fashion statement.

Perhaps you wear a cross or have a cross tattooed somewhere on your body. You wear it proudly as a sign of your allegiance to Jesus Christ. I applaud you. My story is not intended to criticize you, but I do want you to think about why you wear a cross and what it communicates to others. And I want you to think about why others wear a cross and what they intend to communicate (or not communicate) by it.

What is the cross all about anyway?

We will see that it's not about being a cross-wearer.

Jesus demands that we be a cross-bearer.

In a summary of what the gospel is, Paul focuses on the following points:

> Now I make known to you, brethren, the gospel which
> I preached to you, which also you received, in which also
> you stand, by which also you are saved, if you hold fast
> the word which I preached to you, unless you believed in
> vain. For I delivered to you as of first importance what I
> also received, that Christ died for our sins according to
> the Scriptures, and that He was buried, and that He was
> raised on the third day according to the Scriptures, and
> that He appeared to Cephas [Peter], then to the twelve.
> After that He appeared to more than five hundred breth-
> ren at one time, most of whom remain until now, but
> some have fallen asleep; then He appeared to James, then
> to all the apostles; and last of all, as to one untimely
> born, He appeared to me also. (1 Cor. 15:1–8 NASB)

The death, burial, and resurrection of Jesus are the crucial points of the gospel. In this chapter, I want to concentrate on the first two elements—Jesus' death and burial. In the next chapter I will focus on the resurrection. As I talk about the death of Jesus, I will show you how *God the Father* put His own Son to death. (Yes, you read that correctly!) I will show you how *Satan* worked his evil, diaboli-cal influence to kill Jesus. I will show you how people like Jesus' *close friend Judas* and His *enemy Pontius Pilate* conspired together to crucify Jesus.

I'm going to tell you the story of the cross.

Toward the Cross

Throughout His three-year earthly ministry, Jesus headed resolutely toward the cross. On several occasions, He announced to His disciples His God-appointed destiny (as previously mentioned in chap. 5). For example, after Peter openly recognized that Jesus was the Son of God, "from that time on Jesus began to explain to his disciples that he must go to Jerusalem and suffer many things at the hands of the elders, chief priests and teachers of the law, and that he must be killed and on the third day be raised to life" (Matt. 16:21 NIV).

Scripture guided Him in these predictions, as He explained to His followers: "'How unwise and slow you are to believe in your hearts all that the prophets have spoken! Didn't the Messiah have to suffer these things and enter into His glory?' Then beginning with Moses and all the Prophets, He interpreted for them the things concerning Himself in all the Scriptures" (Luke 24:25–27).

Jesus was also conscious that the Father's will for His earthly ministry would culminate in His "hour." While He taught, healed, proclaimed the gospel, exorcised demons, discipled, prayed, obeyed the Father, and overcame temptation, Jesus knew that His time had not yet come. As the three years neared their end, however, Jesus spoke openly about His hour finally arriving. As the time of His death drew closer, Jesus felt more and more distressed by its wretched prospects. "Now My soul is troubled. What should I say—'Father, save Me from this hour'? But that is why I came to this hour" (John 12:27). His enemies, His friends, His own fears, His own will—nothing could deter Jesus from fulfilling what was prophesied and appointed for Him: death. "Jesus resolutely set out for Jerusalem" (Luke 9:51 NIV), moving expectantly and willingly toward the cross.

Above and beyond the Cross

Jesus' decisive march toward His predicted destiny underscores the presence of an unseen reality above and beyond the seemingly tragic events leading up to the cross and His burial. This hidden reality was the eternal plan of God Himself. Before the world was created, the Father had already designed the death of His Son for the salvation of humanity. Indeed Christ was intended to be the perfect sacrificial lamb for us "before the foundation of the world" (1 Pet. 1:20). So the crucifixion of Christ upon the cross was no afterthought, or plan B, but was God's purpose from all eternity. This is why the early Christians could say that Jesus was "delivered up according to God's determined plan and foreknowledge" (Acts 2:23) so that His enemies, in crucifying Christ, fulfilled what God's "hand and . . . plan had predestined to take place" (Acts 4:28).

As we talk about the specific events of Jesus' crucifixion—the plot of His enemies, Judas's betrayal, Herod's clowning, the beating ordered by Pilate, the religious leaders' mocking, the execution by the Roman soldiers, the burial in Joseph's tomb—we must never lose sight of the divine plan that was being enacted and accomplished through these tragic events. God Himself ordained that His Son would be crucified; this reality stands above and beyond the cross.

For the Cross

Judas, Pilate, Herod, the Jewish leaders, and the soldiers constituted an unusual group that championed the crucifixion of Jesus; they were the co-conspirators who were for the cross. Throughout His ministry, many of the Jewish religious leaders—the Pharisees, priests, elders, scribes, lawyers—had opposed Jesus and even threatened to destroy Him. These threats became more frequent and resolute as His ministry progressed. Finally, they coalesced into a concrete plan just days before an important Jewish feast—the Passover. Jesus "said to his disciples, 'As you know, the Passover is two days away—and the Son of Man will be handed over to be crucified.' Then the chief priests and the elders of the people assembled in the palace of the high priest, whose name was Caiaphas, and they plotted to arrest Jesus in some sly way and kill him. 'But not during the Feast,' they said, 'or there may be a riot among the people'" (Matt. 26:1–5 NIV).

This devious plot involved one of Jesus' own friends: "Then one of the Twelve—the one called Judas Iscariot—went to the chief priests and asked, 'What are you willing to give me if I hand him over to you?' So they counted out for him thirty pieces of silver coins. From then on Judas watched for an opportunity to hand him over" (Matt. 26:14–16 NIV).

Jesus was not caught off guard by His opportunistic friend. Indeed, as the disciples were celebrating the first Lord's Supper, Jesus announced that one of them would betray Him and that, for this, a terrible price would be paid: "'Woe to that man who betrays the Son of Man! It would be better for him if he had not been born.' Then Judas, the one who would betray him, said, 'Surely not I, Rabbi?' Jesus answered, 'Yes, it is you'" (Matt. 26:24–25 NIV).

This opportunity presented itself to Judas as Jesus was returning from His prayer time in the garden of Gethsemane. Because the disciples had often met with Jesus in that location, Judas counted on the fact that he could find Jesus there (Luke 22:39; John 18:2). "Judas, one of the Twelve, arrived. With him was a large crowd armed with swords and clubs, sent from the chief priests and the elders of the people. Now the betrayer had arranged a signal with them: 'The one I kiss is the man; arrest him.' Going at once to Jesus, Judas said, 'Greetings, Rabbi!' and kissed him. Jesus replied, 'Friend, do what you came for.' Then the men stepped forward, seized Jesus and arrested him" (Matt. 26:47–50 NIV).

The first stop after Jesus' arrest was for questioning by Annas, Caiaphas, and the high council of the Jews, called the Sanhedrin. Annas was the elderly father of several Jewish high priests. He himself had held that office and apparently continued to exert a great deal of influence over the religious matters of the time. After questioning Jesus (John 18:19–24), Annas sent Him bound in chains to his son-in-law, Caiaphas.

As the reigning high priest, Caiaphas conducted Jesus before the Sanhedrin, the Jewish council that decided religious and legal issues for the people. Putting Jesus on trial before the Sanhedrin so He could be executed required witnesses who could testify that Jesus had broken the law. Though many people came forward, none could offer credible evidence of Jesus' guilt. Finally, Caiaphas himself addressed Jesus:

"I charge you under oath by the living God: Tell us
if you are the Christ, the Son of God." "Yes, it is as you
say," Jesus replied. "But I say to all of you: In the future

> you will see the Son of Man sitting at the right hand of
> the Mighty One and coming on the clouds of heaven."
> Then the high priest tore his clothes and said, "He has
> spoken blasphemy! Why do we need any more witnesses?
> Look, now you have heard the blasphemy. What do you
> think?" "He is worthy of death," they answered. (Matt.
> 26:63–66 NIV)

Blasphemy was the charge against Jesus; that is, He, being a human being, claimed to be God. The Sanhedrin heard Jesus' (supposed) blasphemy, and they pronounced their verdict: Execute Him!

Because the Jews were ruled by the Romans, they did not possess the right to execute anyone according to their religious law. For that, the Sanhedrin had to appeal to the Roman officers in charge. So the next stop for Jesus was Pontius Pilate, the Roman governor.

The Jewish leaders bound Jesus, brought Him to Pilate, and made accusations against Him to demonstrate their case for His execution. But Jesus refused to reply to their charges—an action that confused Pilate. When he learned that Jesus was from Galilee, an area under the rule of Herod, Pilate extradited Him to the proper jurisdiction. Having heard about Jesus' supernatural powers, Herod attempted to induce Jesus to perform a miracle for him. Jesus refused to comply with his new interrogator. Reduced to clowning around with Jesus, Herod dressed Him as a king and ushered Him back to Pilate.

A major obstacle arose at this point: "Pilate called together the chief priests, the rulers and the people, and said to them, 'You brought me this man as one who was inciting the people to rebellion. I have examined him in your presence and have found no basis for your charges against him. Neither has Herod, for he sent him back to us; as you can see, he has done nothing to deserve death. Therefore, I will punish him and then release him'" (Luke 23:13–16 NIV).

So Pilate recognized that Jesus was innocent. In addition, his wife warned him not to take any action against Jesus: "Don't have anything to do with that innocent man, for I have suffered a great deal today in a dream because of him" (Matt. 27:19 NIV). Despite this, Pilate wanted to please the crowds (who had been persuaded to ask Pilate to execute Jesus), so he offered the people a choice.

Now it was the custom at the Feast to release a pris-
oner whom the people requested. A man called Barabbas
was in prison with the insurrectionists who had committed murder in the uprising. The crowd came up and
asked Pilate to do for them what he usually did. "Do you
want me to release to you the king of the Jews?" asked
Pilate, knowing it was out of envy that the chief priests
had handed Jesus over to him. But the chief priests
stirred up the crowd to have Pilate release Barabbas instead. "What shall I do, then, with the one you call the
king of the Jews?" Pilate asked them. "Crucify him!"
they shouted. "Why? What crime has he committed?"
asked Pilate. But they shouted all the louder, "Crucify
him!" Wanting to satisfy the crowd, Pilate released
Barabbas to them. He had Jesus flogged, and handed him
over to be crucified. (Mark 15:6–15 NIV)

As if to clear himself from any and all involvement in Jesus' death,
Pilate "took water and washed his hands in front of the crowd. 'I
am innocent of this man's blood,' he said. 'It is your responsibility!'" (Matt. 27:24 NIV).

Judas, Annas, Caiaphas, the Jewish leaders of the Sanhedrin,
Pilate, Herod, and the crowds together put Jesus to death. But another major player, acting behind the scenes, was also for the cross.
Satan himself exerted a diabolically evil influence in the crucifixion
of Jesus. He did so by entering into Judas (Luke 22:3)—a difficult
feat to imagine, since Jesus Himself had handpicked His disciples.
As He told the apostles: "Have I not chosen you, the Twelve? Yet
one of you [Judas] is a devil!" (John 6:70 NIV).

This satanic influence over Judas was particularly pronounced
immediately before the disciples' celebration of the Passover dinner: "The evening meal was being served, and the devil had already
prompted Judas Iscariot, son of Simon, to betray Jesus" (John 13:2
NIV). Then, when Jesus dipped His piece of bread in a bowl and
gave it to His friend, "as soon as Judas took the bread, Satan entered into him" (John 13:27 NIV). Thus, Satan and his destructive
powers, working through Judas, was for the cross.

Against the Cross

As much as the enemies of Jesus were for the cross, His disciples were against the cross, not wanting their friend and master to die. This opposition to Jesus' divine destiny first arose after
Peter openly professed that Jesus was the Son of God. Though this
realization was not the product of Peter's own insight or human
wisdom but was instead revealed to him by God, Peter quickly and
embarrassingly set himself against God's design for Jesus:

> From that time on Jesus began to explain to his disci-
> ples that he must go to Jerusalem and suffer many things
> at the hands of the elders, chief priests and teachers of
> the law, and that he must be killed and on the third day
> be raised to life. Peter took him aside and began to re-
> buke him. "Never, Lord!" he said. "This shall never hap-
> pen to you!" Jesus turned and said to Peter, "Get behind
> me, Satan! You are a stumbling block to me; you do not
> have in mind the things of God, but the things of men."
> (Matt. 16:21–23 NIV)

Certainly, the reluctance of Peter to see his friend dragged away
to His death is understandable, even admirable. But Jesus could
not stand for such sentimentality. He did not attempt to gently
correct His friend, but violently blasted Peter's notion instead. The
disciples, by being against the cross, were against the will of God
as well.

Away from the Cross

Perhaps their close proximity to Jesus clouded the disciples'
thoughts at the time of their friend's impending death. By the time
of Jesus' crucifixion, however, almost all the disciples had fled away
from the cross. Indeed, this occurred exactly as Jesus predicted it
would in a conversation with them following the Passover dinner:

> Then Jesus told them, "This very night you will all
> fall away on account of me, for it is written, 'I will
> strike the shepherd, and the sheep of the flock will be
> scattered.' But after I have risen, I will go ahead of you
> into Galilee." Peter replied, "Even if all fall away on ac-
> count of you, I never will." "I tell you the truth," Jesus
> answered, "this very night, before the rooster crows, you

will disown me three times." But Peter declared, "Even if
I have to die with you, I will never disown you." And all
the disciples said the same. (Matt. 26:31–35 NIV)

Professing their loyalty for their master was one thing; carrying through on their promise to die for Him was another. For
example, while in the courtyard of Caiaphas during Jesus' interrogation by the high priest, Peter was questioned three times about
his association with Jesus:

Now Peter was sitting out in the courtyard, and a
servant girl came to him. "You also were with Jesus of
Galilee," she said. But he denied it before them all. "I
don't know what you're talking about," he said. Then
he went out to the gateway, where another girl saw him
and said to the people there, "This fellow was with Jesus
of Nazareth." He denied it again, with an oath: "I don't
know the man!" After a little while, those standing there
went up to Peter and said, "Surely you are one of them,
for your accent gives you away." Then he began to call
down curses on himself and he swore to them, "I don't
know the man!" Immediately a rooster crowed. Then
Peter remembered the word Jesus had spoken: "Before
the rooster crows, you will disown me three times." And
he went outside and wept bitterly. (Matt. 26:69–75 NIV)

With similar denial, and out of a sense of great fear, all of the disciples abandoned Jesus. As they left their friend to die alone, the
disciples moved away from the cross.

To the Cross

Judas' kiss, Herod's interrogation, the Sanhedrin's verdict, the
crowd's demand for Barabbas—the actions of Christ's betrayers
dovetailed together. As the next step in the drama, Pilate sentenced
Jesus to the cross, then turned Him over to the Roman soldiers:

After having Jesus scourged, he [Pilate] handed Him
over to be crucified. Then the soldiers of the governor
took Jesus into the Praetorium and gathered the whole
Roman cohort around Him. They stripped Him and put a
scarlet robe on him. And after twisting together a crown
of thorns, they put it on His head, and a reed in His right

hand; and they knelt down before Him and mocked
Him, saying, "Hail, King of the Jews!" They spat on Him,
and took the reed and began to beat Him on the head.
After they had mocked Him, they took the scarlet robe
off Him and put His own garments back on Him, and
led Him away to crucify Him. (Matt. 27:26–31 NASB)

As He moved from the guardhouse to the place of execution, Jesus was
required to carry a piece of wood that would become the horizontal
bar of the cross on which He would be crucified. Apparently having
been overcome with exhaustion and humiliation as a result of being
beaten and mocked, Jesus was unable to fulfill His responsibility:

As they were coming out, they found a man of Cyrene
named Simon, whom they pressed into service to bear His
cross. And when they came to a place called Golgotha,
which means Place of a Skull, they gave Him wine to
drink mixed with gall [supposedly to help kill His pain];
and after tasting it, He was unwilling to drink. And when
they had crucified Him, they divided up His garments
among themselves by casting lots. And sitting down, they
began to keep watch over Him there. And above His head
they put up the charge against Him which read, "This is
Jesus the King of the Jews." (Matt. 27:32–37 NASB)

Crucifixion was a common means of executing criminals in the
ancient world—it was an awful, excruciatingly painful manner of
death. Jesus' arms were secured to the wooden bar by nails driven
through His wrists. This piece was then hoisted and affixed to a
vertical piece of wood that had been driven into the ground. So
that His legs would be bent at the knees, Jesus' feet were also nailed
to the vertical piece. According to the conventions of Jesus' day, the
time of His crucifixion was the third hour of the day—about nine
o'clock in the morning.

Pilate and the Roman soldiers were the ones who sentenced
and nailed Jesus to the cross.

PAUSE TIME

In conjunction with Mel Gibson's movie *The Passion of the
Christ*, a heated discussion arose concerning the question, Who
put Jesus to death? Some people were fearful that the movie

blamed the Jews for Christ's death. From this chapter, how would you answer that question? If your response contains multiple names (as it should), how does this complex answer help you to share with your friends that every person needs Jesus Christ?

Around the Cross

Though most of His disciples abandoned Him, some members of His family and some supporters of His ministry did not scatter but gathered around the cross: "Many women were there looking on from a distance, who had followed Jesus from Galilee while ministering to Him. Among them was Mary Magdalene, and Mary the mother of James and Joseph, and the mother of the sons of Zebedee" (Matt. 27:55–56 NASB).

Furthermore, Jesus' mother, Mary, and His close disciple John were present at the crucifixion: "Standing by the cross of Jesus were His mother, His mother's sister, Mary the wife of Clopas, and Mary Magdalene. When Jesus saw His mother and the disciple He loved standing there, He said to His mother, 'Woman, here is your son.' Then He said to the disciple, 'Here is your mother.' And from that hour the disciple took her into his home" (John 19:25–27). One of Jesus' last acts was to provide for His mother after His death. As the oldest son of Mary, He bore the responsibility for her in case she was widowed; apparently, Joseph had died by this time. Linking His mother with John His beloved disciple, Jesus made sure that she would be taken care of. At His crucifixion, Jesus' mother, several women supporters, and His disciple John were with Him around the cross.

On the Cross

While these women wept for Him, the other members of the crowd mocked and ridiculed Jesus as He hung on the cross.

Those passing by were hurling abuse at Him, wagging their heads and saying, "You who are going to destroy the temple and rebuild it in three days, save Yourself! If You are the Son of God, come down from the cross." In the same way the chief priests also, along with the scribes and elders, were mocking Him and saying, "He

saved others; He cannot save Himself. He is the King of
Israel; let Him now come down from the cross, and we
will believe in Him. He trusts in God; let God rescue
Him now, if He delights in Him; for He said, 'I am the
Son of God.'" (Matt. 27:39–43 NASB)

Let's take a moment to analyze these insults hurled at Jesus:

- Was Jesus the Son of God? Certainly! But He could not
  come down from the cross and accomplish what He the
  Son had been sent by the Father to do.
- Did Jesus save others? Absolutely! But He could not save
  Himself and save others at the same time. So He chose not
  to save Himself, though He could have.
- Did Jesus trust in God, and did the Father take pleasure in
  Him? Totally! But God could not deliver His Son and de-
  liver us at the same time. So the Father left His Son to die.

Along with the excruciating physical pain, Jesus also had to endure
these insults from the soldiers, the passersby, and the religious
leaders.

Two thieves crucified at the same time next to Him also taunted
Jesus. Then something happened:

One of the criminals who were hanged there was
hurling abuse at Him, saying, "Are You not the Christ?
Save Yourself and us!" But the other answered and re-
buking him said, "Do you not even fear God, since you
are under the same sentence of condemnation? And we
indeed are suffering justly, for we are receiving what
we deserve for our deeds; but this man has done nothing wrong." And he was saying, "Jesus, remember me
when You come in Your kingdom!" And [Jesus] said to
him, "Truly I say to you, today you shall be with Me in
Paradise." (Luke 23:39–43 NASB)

Clearly, this second crucified criminal recognized several things:
the innocence of Jesus (Jesus was not being crucified because He
had committed any crime), the rightness of his own punishment
(he was indeed guilty of condemnation), and Jesus' authority to
save him. So while hanging on the cross, Jesus forgave the second
thief and promised him life after death.

As Jesus hung on the cross, it became increasingly difficult for Him to breathe, suffocation being the main cause of death during crucifixion. The shock, hunger, thirst, sheer exhaustion, and loss of blood hastened His death. His final thoughts were directed toward the Father. Though He, the innocent Son of God, was being executed by guilt-laden sinners, Jesus prayed, "Father, forgive them, because they do not know what they are doing" (Luke 23:34).

As He bore the horrendous weight of the furious wrath of the Father against the sins of the world, "about three in the afternoon Jesus cried out with a loud voice, '*Eli, Eli, lema sabachthani?*' that is, 'My God, My God, why have You forsaken Me?'" (Matt. 27:46). As difficult as it may seem to us, the Father punished His own Son. He condemned Jesus for our sins and separated Himself from this object of His bitter hatred. And so Jesus experienced an alienation from His own Father that He had never before suffered.

The bystanders, hearing Jesus cry out words in Aramaic (this was Jesus' primary language, though the Roman soldiers spoke Greek), misunderstood Him: "When some of those standing there heard this, they said, 'He's calling for Elijah!' Immediately one of them ran and got a sponge, filled it with sour wine, fixed it on a reed, and offered Him a drink. But the rest said, 'Let's see if Elijah comes to save Him'" (Matt. 27:47–49). This drink offering was futile, for six hours hanging on the cross was too much suffering for Him. "Jesus called out with a loud voice, 'Father, into Your hands I entrust My spirit.' Saying this, He breathed His last" (Luke 23:46).

It was the ninth hour, or about three o'clock in the afternoon, when Jesus died on the cross.

Down from the Cross

Jesus' lifeless body needed to be taken down from the cross. This was especially important because of the Jewish Sabbath law:

> The Jews, because it was the day of preparation, so that the bodies would not remain on the cross on the Sabbath (for that Sabbath was a high day), asked Pilate that their legs might be broken, and that they might be taken away. So the soldiers came, and broke the legs of the first man and of the other who was crucified with

Him; but coming to Jesus, when they saw that He was
already dead, they did not break His legs. But one of the
soldiers pierced His side with a spear, and immediately
blood and water came out. (John 19:31–34 NASB)

Soldiers would break the legs of those being crucified to prevent
them from using their feet—which were nailed to the cross—to
thrust themselves up so as to breathe. With broken legs, suffocation was nearly immediate; thus, the two thieves crucified with
Jesus died soon afterward. But Jesus was already dead. Six hours
of painful physical suffering, together with the spiritual torment
of bearing the punishment for the sins of the world, were all that
Jesus could endure. The flow of blood and water from His pierced
side confirmed that Jesus was indeed dead.

But Jesus' body still needed to be buried. Joseph of Arimathea,
a member of the Sanhedrin—he did not agree with their decision
to execute Jesus (Luke 23:50–51)—yet also a secret disciple, approached Pilate and requested the body of Jesus. Pilate consented,
and Joseph took the body down from the cross to place it in a
tomb.

He was joined in this by Nicodemus, who brought "a mixture
of myrrh and aloes, about a hundred pounds weight. So they took
the body of Jesus and bound it in linen wrappings with the spices,
as is the burial custom of the Jews" (John 19:39–40 NASB). This
fragrant potpourri would mask the stench that would soon be
emitted from Jesus' decaying body. Then Joseph "laid it in his own
new tomb, which he had hewn out in the rock; and he rolled a
large stone against the entrance of the tomb and went away. And
Mary Magdalene was there, and the other Mary, sitting opposite
the grave" (Matt. 27:60–61 NASB).

Jesus' body was taken down from the cross and deposited in a
tomb.

"For I delivered to you as of first importance what I also received, that Christ died for our sins according to the Scriptures,
and that He was buried" (1 Cor. 15:3–4 NASB).

At the Cross

So now we know the major characters and events at the crucifixion of Jesus Christ: the religious leaders, Judas, the disciples,

Annas, Caiaphas, Herod, Pontius Pilate, the Roman soldiers, the crowds of people.

Only one more major player remains.

You.

You are at the cross.

What does the cross mean for you?

Jesus' work in dying on the cross and accomplishing our salvation is often referred to as the *atonement*. In one sense, the atonement encompasses all of Jesus' life as well as His death, because His perfect obedience during His life was a necessary part of accomplishing our salvation. Apart from His sinless, perfect life, Jesus could not have died on the cross for our sins. For our purposes, however, I will focus on the atonement as the work Jesus did by dying on the cross to obtain our salvation.

The atonement vividly exhibits two attributes of God: His love and His justice. It was God's love for us that prompted Him to send Jesus to make atonement for our sins: "For while we were still helpless, at the right time Christ died for the ungodly. For one will hardly die for a righteous man; though perhaps for the good man someone would dare even to die. But God demonstrates His own love toward us, in that while we were yet sinners, Christ died for us" (Rom. 5:6–8 NASB).

God saw us in our miserable ruin and, full of loving compassion, sent Christ to die for us. Certainly, this was not due to our goodness and nice behavior. On the contrary, God's love reached out to us while we were still alienated from Him. While we were still sinners, Christ died for us.

Sometimes we may wonder why God, in loving us, didn't just befriend us and spare His Son such agonizing suffering and horrendous death on the cross. Why didn't God just forgive us and skip the rest? God's justice demanded that atonement be made for our sins. God, being perfectly holy, cannot tolerate sin. Wherever sin is found, God must deal with it by punishing it. God's justice must be satisfied before He can involve Himself in a relationship with us.

According to God's own law, the penalty for sin is death—both physical death and spiritual separation from Him for all eternity. God would have been just if He made us pay the penalty for our sins: we would die and be condemned forever and that would be just. However, God offers us a way of escape—Jesus died in our place and paid the penalty for our sins. His death for sins satisfied the justice of God. Jesus died physically and was separated from the Father in our place. Thus, God is completely just—sin is punished in the death of Christ—and also completely loving—He brings us into a personal relationship with Himself through Jesus.

Christ's atonement is a *penal substitutionary* work. Christ paid the penalty for our sins by dying on the cross in our place—as our substitute. At the cross, the love and justice of God wonderfully meet and are perfectly expressed!

Let's go deeper still: We may imagine the work of Christ on the cross as a multifaceted diamond. Each facet represents a different aspect of Christ's atoning work, but viewed together the facets help us to understand how incredibly rich His work really is.

The first facet has already been introduced: Christ paid the penalty that we deserved to pay. So the atonement was a sacrifice. Specifically, the death of Jesus was a *sacrifice of expiation*. This means that Christ paid the penalty for our sin and guilt and so removed our liability or obligation to suffer punishment. The Old Testament sacrifices—time and time again the priests offered the sacrifices of slaughtered bulls and goats—were expiatory. However, "In those sacrifices there is a reminder of sins year by year. For it is impossible for the blood of bulls and goats to take away sins. . . . Every priest stands daily ministering and offering time after time the same sacrifices, which can never take away sins; but He [Jesus], having offered one sacrifice for sins for all time, sat down at the right hand of God" (Heb. 10:3-4, 11-12).

Jesus' sacrifice is a once-and-for-all sacrifice. It never has to be repeated. Why? First, because He was the perfect high priest to mediate between God and us: "For this is the kind of high priest we need: holy, innocent, undefiled, separated from sinners, and exalted above the heavens. He doesn't need to offer sacrifices every day, as high priests do—first for their own sins, then for those of the people. He did this once for all when He offered Himself" (Heb. 7:26-28). Second, because He is our eternal high priest: "Now many have become [Levitical] priests, since they are prevented by death from remaining in office. But because He remains forever,

He holds his priesthood permanently. Therefore He is always able to save those who come to God through Him, since He always lives to intercede for them" (Heb. 7:23–25).

Third, Jesus never has to repeat His sacrifice because He offered His own life in sacrifice for us: "He entered the holy of holies once for all, not by the blood of goats and calves, but by His own blood, having obtained eternal redemption. For if the blood of goats and bulls and the ashes of a heifer sprinkling those who are defiled, sanctify for the purification of the flesh, how much more will the blood of the Messiah, who through the eternal Spirit offered Himself without blemish to God, cleanse our consciences from dead works to serve the living God?" (Heb. 9:12–14). The remarkable thing about Jesus' sacrifice, in contrast with all those animal sacrifices offered by the priests, was that He offered His own life. Furthermore, He made one sacrifice that never has to be repeated. He died once for all time, and He never has to die again. His atonement was a sacrifice of expiation.

The second facet: Christ experienced the wrath of God that we deserved to experience. So the atonement is a *propitiation*. In the Old Testament, the blood of bulls and goats was spread on an altar so as to cover the sins of God's people. As God observed this propitiation, He saw the covering rather than the sin itself. Thus, God's wrath due to sin was appeased. Similarly, Christ's death was a propitiation: "Love consists in this: not that we loved God, but that He loved us and sent His Son to be the propitiation for our sins" (1 John 4:10). In so doing, God's wrath was turned away from us—we will never face it. The atonement was a propitiation.

The third facet: Christ removed the enmity and separation between God and us; thus, the atonement accomplishes *reconciliation*. We were once enemies of God. By the cross of Jesus, we are brought into friendship with Him: "For if, while we were enemies, we were reconciled to God through the death of His Son, [then how] much more, having been reconciled, will we be saved by His life!" (Rom. 5:10). Through reconciliation, we have become the friends of God.

The fourth facet: Christ freed us from slavery to sin through His forgiveness. So the atonement brings *redemption*. This aspect of the atonement portrays us as slaves, sold into bondage to sin. Our disobedience, indifference, rebellion, and faithlessness formed a four-walled prison in which we were bound. And we were powerless to escape from our sinful life by ourselves. Here is where Jesus worked His redemption, as He Himself said: "the Son of Man did not come to be served, but to serve, and to give His life—a ransom for many" (Mark 10:45). A ransom is the price that is paid to release a slave from prison. And we "were bought at a price" (1 Cor. 6:20)—the blood of Christ: "you were not redeemed with perishable things like silver or gold from your futile way of life inherited from your forefathers, but with precious blood, as of a lamb unblemished and spotless, the blood of Christ" (1 Pet. 1:18–19 NASB). Through redemption, we are free from sin.

Expiatory sacrifice. Propitiation. Reconciliation. Redemption. Four facets of the *atonement*, Christ's work of dying on the cross on our behalf, to pay the *penalty* for our sins as our *substitute*. When we turn from our sin and embrace Jesus Christ, the atonement satisfies the justice of God, turns away God's wrath, brings us into friendship with God, and frees us from slavery to sin.

This is what the cross of Christ accomplished for us.

PAUSE TIME

And what does Jesus ask of us in return?

"If anyone would come after me, he must deny himself and take up his cross and follow me" (Matt. 16:24 NIV).

Jesus calls us to be His disciples. We must deny ourselves—forsake our own agenda, yield the control of our life, relinquish our own will—and follow Jesus—take our orders from Him, submit to Him, obey Him, accomplish His will.

This is what it means to take up our cross. On the cross, Jesus died. As those who take up our own cross, we too must die—to our own selves.

The cross is all about death.

You see, it's not about being cross-wearers.

Jesus demands that we be cross-bearers.

CHAPTER SEVEN

BREAKING THE POWER OF DEATH

Nonantola is a small city in north central Italy. It is well known for its rich agriculture and grazing lands and its highly developed food industry. This agricultural and industrial development is due to a political factor: Nonantola is thoroughly controlled by the Communist Party of Italy. It was the Communists who, in the middle part of the last century, took over the city and began to transform it into a prosperous and wealthy area.

As staff members of Campus Crusade for Christ working in Italy, my wife and I had a wonderful opportunity to help direct an evangelistic campaign in Nonantola. Along with a group of about two dozen other Christians, we went door to door and visited every family in the city, engaging in many conversations about Jesus Christ. We held rallies in the church, hosted events in the parks, and even (briefly) took over the local dance club to share Christ using the DJ's microphone.

Toward what we projected to be the end of our campaign, we got word that Giorgio, a key Communist labor union leader, was boasting that no one from our group had yet contacted him. He assumed this meant we were all afraid of him. When Nora and I heard this, we headed straight over to Giorgio's house and sat down with him in his living room. He explained that the problems of the world are all economic and political: most political systems are corrupt and therefore don't function to help people; most people are poor and don't have access to jobs that will help them out of poverty; most nations are locked in a vicious cycle of political and economic failure; and so forth. Solve these problems and you will solve the problems of mankind, Giorgio proudly urged.

But, we countered, having spent a week with the people of his city, we had come to learn that what they desired most of all was love, deep relationships, family harmony, fair treatment of others, a sense of meaning and purpose to life, and other such intangible realities. Also, we informed him that several hundred of his townspeople had joined weekly Bible studies to know more about Jesus Christ. This pointed out to us, we told Giorgio, that the deepest needs of people are spiritual ones, not political and economic problems.

This turned our entire conversation around.

For nearly two hours, we moved closer and closer to the heart of the good news about Jesus Christ. Then an amazing thing happened.

Giorgio admitted to us why he is not a Christian.

He did not—and could not—believe in the resurrection of Jesus Christ.

How far we had progressed in those two hours! From a discussion of political and economic woes to a frank admission about rejection of the resurrection.

Now that is something with which Nora and I could effectively deal.

––––

Why does the resurrection of Jesus Christ play such an important role in Christianity, so that rejection of the resurrection means rejection of Jesus as Savior and Lord?

Remember what Paul said about the essence of the gospel:

> Now I make known to you, brethren, the gospel
> which I preached to you, which also you received, in
> which also you stand, by which also you are saved, if you
> hold fast the word which I preached to you, unless you
> believed in vain. For I delivered to you as of first impor-
> tance what I also received, that Christ died for our sins
> according to the Scriptures, and that He was buried,
> and that He was raised on the third day according to the

Scriptures, and that He appeared to Cephas [Peter], then
to the twelve. After that He appeared to more than five
hundred brethren at one time, most of whom remain
until now, but some have fallen asleep; then He appeared to James, then to all the apostles; and last of all,
as to one untimely born, He appeared to me also. (1 Cor.
15:1-8 NASB)

This is the gospel: that Jesus Christ died, was buried, and on the
third day rose from the dead. In the last chapter, I concentrated
on the first two elements: Jesus' death and burial. In this chapter,
I will focus on the resurrection. A person cannot embrace the gospel, cannot know Jesus as Savior and Lord, cannot be His disciple
without believing in His resurrection.

How did the resurrection of Jesus come about?

Absolutely, Positively, Undeniably, Completely Dead(?)

Immediately after Jesus' crucifixion and burial, wild rumors
began to spread about Him. As if His enemies had not already done
enough in executing Him, some of those same conspirators gathered together to ensure that no one could make it appear that Jesus
rose from the dead:

Now on the next day, the day after the preparation,
the chief priests and the Pharisees gathered together with
Pilate, and said, "Sir, we remember that when He was
still alive that deceiver said, 'After three days I am to rise
again.' Therefore, give orders for the grave to be made
secure until the third day, otherwise His disciples may
come and steal Him away and say to the people, 'He has
risen from the dead,' and the last deception will be worse
than the first." Pilate said to them, "You have a guard;
go, make it as secure as you know how." And they went
and made the grave secure, and along with the guard
they set a seal on the stone. (Matt. 27:62-66 NASB)

Jesus was dead and buried. Still, His enemies stationed a police
guard around the tomb and affixed a seal to the large stone covering its entrance (the penalty for breaking such an official seal

was death). Every precaution was taken to keep Jesus' body in the tomb.

On the Third Day

How ironic is the scene above! The enemies of Jesus recalled that while He was still alive, Jesus had prophesied His resurrection on the third day following His death. As a consequence, His enemies did something about His prediction. Such was not the case, however, with Jesus' friends. Though on several occasions they had heard Jesus announce His resurrection, not one of them believed Him.

So Jesus' enemies feared that His words would come true—even if only a phony resurrection perpetrated by His supporters—while His friends gave up all hope following Jesus' death. Go figure!

Their complete hopelessness was exemplified by a group of Jesus' female followers. Immediately after His death, they set about preparing more spices and perfumes with which they would anoint Jesus' entombed corpse; these would further cover up the smell of decay. Normally, the women would have anointed Jesus' body soon after it was laid in the tomb, as Nicodemus and Joseph had done. They were prevented from doing so, however, by a Jewish law: They could do no work—this included anointing dead bodies—from sunset on Friday to sunset on Saturday in order to observe the Sabbath.

So they waited until Sunday. "When the Sabbath was over, Mary Magdalene, and Mary the mother of James and Salome, bought spices, so that they might come and anoint Him. Very early on the first day of the week, they came to the tomb when the sun had risen. They were saying to one another, 'Who will roll away the stone for us from the entrance of the tomb?'" (Mark 16:1–3 NASB).

Though ready with the spices, the women anticipated that they would face an insurmountable obstacle. So they approached Jesus' tomb with deep concern. "And they found the stone rolled away from the tomb" (Luke 24:2 NASB). Certainly they were shocked and wondered how the stone had been displaced! "A severe earthquake had occurred, for an angel of the Lord descended from heaven and came and rolled away the stone and sat upon it. And his appearance was like lightning, and his clothing as white as snow. The guards shook for fear of him and became like dead men" (Matt. 28:2–4 NASB). With the stone having been rolled away and the guards scattered from fear, the women entered the tomb.

But when they entered, they did not find the body of the Lord Jesus. While they were perplexed about this, behold, two men suddenly stood near them in dazzling clothing; and as the women were terrified and bowed their faces to the ground, the men said to them, "Why do you seek the living One among the dead? He is not here, but He has risen. Remember how He spoke to you while He was still in Galilee, saying that the Son of Man must be delivered into the hands of sinful men, and be crucified, and the third day rise again." And they remembered His words, and returned from the tomb and reported all these things to the eleven and to all the rest. (Luke 24:3–9 NASB)

Clearly, the two "men" who greeted the women in the tomb were angels. They questioned the women's action, underscoring their lack of faith in Jesus' prophecy of His resurrection. So the angels reminded the women of Jesus' prediction. Though they remembered what Jesus had said and reported the morning's events to the disciples, the women were still completely confused. Because grave robbery was quite common, they could imagine only one explanation for the empty tomb. So they filed this report to the disciples: "They have taken away the Lord out of the tomb, and we do not know where they have laid Him" (John 20:2 NASB).

Peter and John decided to check out the tomb for themselves:

The two were running together; and the other disciple ran ahead faster than Peter, and came to the tomb first, and stooping and looking in, he saw the linen wrappings lying there; but he did not go in. And so Simon Peter also came, following him, and entered the tomb; and he saw the linen wrappings lying there, and the face-cloth which had been on His head, not lying with the linen wrappings, but rolled up in a place by itself. So the other disciple who had first come to the tomb then also entered, and he saw and believed. (John 20:4–8 NASB)

Peter and John saw unmistakable evidence that Jesus' body had not been stolen from the tomb. The grave clothes, along with the sizable amount of spices, were still lying there, as if the body of Jesus had just slipped out of them. The facecloth that had been wrapped around Jesus' head was neatly rolled up somewhere else in the tomb, as if Jesus had put it aside because He no longer needed it.

Only one conclusion could be draw from this scene. Whereas crime scene investigators would have hunted for a natural explanation for the scientific evidence, no natural explanation could suffice for what had occurred. Indeed, the disciple John drew the only conclusion possible: Jesus had risen from the dead! And John's belief in the resurrection was based on the evidence—the empty tomb and the grave clothes—not on the Word of God: "For as yet they did not understand the Scripture, that He [Jesus] must rise again from the dead" (John 20:9 NASB). And though John grasped the resurrection because of the evidence that he saw, such was not the case with his companion: Peter "went away, wondering to himself what had happened" (Luke 24:12 NIV).

So John believed, but Peter didn't.

What would persuade the others that Jesus had indeed been raised from the dead?

It would take appearances by Jesus Himself to convince the remaining disciples.

The Post-resurrection Appearances

The first of these appearances was to Mary Magdalene. Returning to the tomb, she first encountered two angels inside: "Mary was standing outside the tomb weeping; and so, as she wept, she stooped and looked into the tomb; and she saw two angels in white sitting, one at the head and one at the feet, where the body of Jesus had been lying. And they said to her, 'Woman, why are you weeping?' She said to them, 'Because they have taken away my Lord, and I do not know where they have laid him'" (John 20:11–13 NASB).

Mary was still of the opinion that grave robbers had snatched the body of Jesus from the tomb. Suddenly, she sensed the presence of someone else near her: "When she had said this, she turned around and saw Jesus standing there, and did not know that it was Jesus. Jesus said to her, 'Woman, why are you weeping? Whom are you seeking?' Supposing Him to be the gardener, she said to Him, 'Sir, if you have carried Him away, tell me where you have laid Him, and I will take Him away.' Jesus said to her, 'Mary!' She turned and said to Him in Hebrew, 'Rabboni!' (which means, Teacher)" (John 20:14–16 NASB).

All Mary wanted was to find the body of Jesus to give Him a proper burial. Not recognizing Jesus in His resurrection body, Mary mistook the person who questioned her; she thought He was the gardener and could help her out. Little did she suspect that Jesus had risen from the dead and was standing face-to-face with her. But as Jesus spoke her name, she immediately recognized Him.

Apparently, Mary then grabbed onto Jesus—certainly out of love and relief. She wanted to hold on to Him for just a few minutes, to enjoy once again His words, His comfort, His friendship. Jesus, however, rebuked her: "Stop clinging to Me, for I have not yet ascended to the Father; but go to My brethren and say to them, 'I ascend to My Father and your Father, and My God and your God'" (John 20:17 NASB). There was no need for Mary to grab onto Jesus, for He had not yet ascended—moved physically—into heaven. Apparently, Jesus would be with her and the disciples for some time before leaving them permanently. So He gave her orders to tell the disciples that He was with them for a while but was going to ascend into heaven at some point. Obeying her teacher and friend, "Mary Magdalene came, announcing to the disciples, 'I have seen the Lord,' and that He had said these things to her" (John 20:18 NASB).

And so began a period between His resurrection from the dead and His ascension into heaven—forty days, during which Jesus appeared regularly to His various followers:

- The two disciples on the road to Emmaus—unable to recognize Jesus, they shared all the events of His death and the reports of the empty tomb, continuing in their blindness until He blessed and broke bread with them at the evening meal (Luke 24:13–33).
- The disciples without Thomas—Jesus proved His identity by showing them the wound marks from His crucifixion; He also launched them on the same mission of the forgiveness of sin on which the Father had sent Him, promising them

the Holy Spirit to empower their work (Luke 24:36-49; John 20:19-23).

- The disciples with Thomas—Jesus allowed His doubting disciple to touch the nail wounds in His wrists and His pierced side, at which Thomas believed (John 20:24-28); then Jesus noted, "Because you have seen Me, have you believed? Blessed are they who did not see, and yet believed" (John 20:29 NASB).

- Seven disciples at the Sea of Tiberius—after directing the group to catch fish, Jesus prepared breakfast for the wearied fishermen; He also commissioned Peter to care for His followers (John 21:15-19).

- More than five hundred followers—this occurred at one appearance; some twenty to thirty years later, most of these eyewitnesses were still living (1 Cor. 15:6).

- James—as Jesus' half brother, he eventually became the leader of the church of Jerusalem (1 Cor. 15:7).

- The apostle Paul—this was years after the period of Jesus' appearances between His resurrection and ascension; Paul realized how unusual this appearance to him was, but it qualified him to be an apostle of Jesus Christ (1 Cor. 15:8-9).

Though each appearance was different, some common elements stand out. Jesus often went unrecognized by those to whom He appeared. Apparently, Jesus' resurrected body was sufficiently different from His pre-crucified body that even those who knew Him intimately did not know Him right away. Alternatively, those who saw His appearance were simply "prevented from recognizing Him" (Luke 24:16).

At times, a critical event had to occur before recognition could take place. This could be Jesus' calling out His follower's name (John 20:16), His blessing and breaking of bread (Luke 24:30-31), His demonstration of the wound marks of His crucifixion (His hands, feet, and pierced side, according to Luke 24:36-40 and John 20:19-20), or His giving of directions for a large catch of fish (John 21:4-7).

Clearly, Jesus' resurrection body possessed supernatural abilities. For example, it simply passed through the grave clothes, leaving the linens, facecloth, and spices in the tomb (John 20:5-7).

Jesus' body also could simply appear in a room, the doors of which were shut tightly (John 20:19, 26)—the resurrected Jesus did not need to walk into a room through its doorways. At the same time, His resurrection body was quite human. Jesus could prepare breakfast for His disciples, cooking fish over a charcoal fire (John 21:9); indeed, Jesus Himself could eat broiled fish (Luke 24:41–43). His body consisted of flesh and bones; clearly, then, He was no mere spirit (Luke 24:36–39) but a physical resurrected person. Because of this, Jesus could invite Thomas to touch the crucifixion wounds still marking His body (John 20:27). Jesus rose in a glorified body that possessed both human and supernatural traits.

Besides proving His resurrection, Jesus' appearances gave Him the opportunity to educate His followers about two pivotal issues. The first was guiding the disciples through "the Law of Moses and the Prophets and the Psalms" (the Old Testament) to explain His and their mission:

> Now He [Jesus] said to them, "These are My words which I spoke to you while I was still with you, that all things which are written about Me in the Law of Moses and the Prophets and the Psalms must be fulfilled." Then He opened their minds to understand the Scriptures, and He said to them, "Thus it is written, that the Christ would suffer and rise again from the dead the third day; and that repentance for forgiveness of sins would be proclaimed in His name to all the nations, beginning from Jerusalem. You are witnesses of these things." (Luke 24:44–48)

The death and resurrection of Jesus Christ were predicted throughout the pages of the Old Testament. During His ministry, Jesus had particularly emphasized that point with His disciples. But those pages contained another prophecy as well: the good news of the forgiveness of sins, received by repentance (or turning from those sins to God), would be communicated throughout the world. Jesus had come to proclaim the gospel and to accomplish what was needed for the forgiveness of sins. Now it fell to His disciples— eyewitnesses of His death, resurrection, proclamation of the good news, and accomplishment of salvation—to further the ministry of the gospel.

This brings us to the second pivotal issue: Jesus giving the Great Commission to His disciples. "And Jesus came up and spoke to them saying, 'All authority has been given to Me in heaven and on earth. Go therefore and make disciples of all the nations, baptizing them in the name of the Father and the Son and the Holy Spirit, teaching them to observe all that I have commanded you; and lo, I am with you always, even to the end of the age'" (Matt. 28:18–20 NASB).

Jesus clarified the future ministry of the disciples. They were to make disciples as they went intentionally throughout the world. Discipleship included baptism into the name of the triune God— Father, Son, and Holy Spirit—and instruction so that Jesus' followers would be obedient to His Word. This Great Commission was backed by the authority of Jesus Himself. And it would be made possible by the enduring presence of Jesus Himself with all those who would carry out His charge.

These post-resurrection appearances continued for a period of forty days. They provided "many convincing proofs" that Jesus was no longer dead but was indeed alive, resurrected from the dead. During this time, Jesus also spoke "of the things concerning the kingdom of God" (Acts 1:3 NASB). He instructed His followers about the kingdom mission on which they were about to be launched.

The Significance of Jesus' Resurrection

The resurrection underscores certain essential truths about Jesus Christ and us as His followers. It demonstrates convincingly that God the Father was pleased by the sacrificial death of His Son for the sins of the world. His pleasure in the sacrifice paved the way for believers to be justified in that sacrifice. Paul wrote about us "who believe in Him [God] who raised Jesus our Lord from the dead" and how Jesus "was raised because of our justification" (Rom. 4:24–25 NASB).

We saw in the last chapter that Jesus died to pay the penalty for our sins. Now we see an additional fact about justification (we'll explore this further later): Jesus was resurrected because God was satisfied by the death of Christ—His sacrificial death fully paid the penalty for our sins such that all our guilt and condemnation has been born by Christ. God considers us to have no more guilt because Jesus took our guilt for us. In a sense, then, by raising Christ from the dead, God publicly placed His seal of approval on His Son's death for our sins.

Moreover, the resurrection assures us that we possess a new and dynamic life—a "resurrection life"—as Christians. Peter prayed, "Blessed be the God and Father of our Lord Jesus Christ, who according to His great mercy has caused us to be born again to a living hope through the resurrection of Jesus Christ from the dead" (1 Pet. 1:3 NASB). Because God powerfully raised His Son, He transforms us, giving us a new life that mirrors the resurrection life of Christ.

That same power that raised Christ from the dead becomes available to us as we live by faith. This is why Paul prays that we might know "what is the surpassing greatness of His [God's] power toward us who believe. These are in accordance with the working of the strength of His might which He brought about in Christ, when He raised Him from the dead and seated Him at His right hand in the heavenly places" (Eph. 1:19-20 NASB). Before embracing Christ, we lived impotent lives, being ensnared in indifference, rebellion, disobedience, and unfaithfulness. As Christians we now possess resurrection power to resist temptation, overcome habitual sinful habits, love God and others, and engage in effective ministry. Indeed, whatever good work God desires for us to do, He always supplies the resources necessary to carry through with it—through the resurrection of Jesus Christ.

Furthermore, the resurrection gives us unshakable hope that we, too, will rise from the dead and live forever with Him. A title that is given to Christ is the "firstborn from the dead" (Col. 1:18); that is, Christ is *only the first* to be resurrected. Many others—all of us who are His followers—will follow Him in resurrection. Paul says something similar when He gives an ordered outline of future events: "in Christ all will be made alive. But each in his own order: Christ, the firstfruits; afterward, at His coming, the people of Christ. Then comes the end" (1 Cor. 15:22-24).

Though all of us Christians will be raised from the dead like Christ, our resurrection will not occur until He returns for the second time. Only then, at His second coming, will our bodies be resurrected: "our citizenship is in heaven, from which we also eagerly wait for a Savior, the Lord Jesus Christ. He will transform the body of our humble condition into the likeness of His glorious body, by the power that enables Him to subject everything to Himself" (Phil. 3:20–21). Like His body, our resurrection bodies will be imperishable, glorious, powerful, and spiritual (1 Cor. 15:42–44). What this means is hard for anyone to say, but I have already placed the order for my resurrected body: six feet eight inches tall, 240 pounds, able to dunk over Michael Jordan!

PAUSE TIME

Consider several issues attached to the resurrection. First, how does the resurrection of Jesus Christ give you assurance that all of your sins, the penalty of death, the judgment of condemnation, and eternal punishment in hell have been removed forever from you? If you will never have to face these realities, how does that fact make you want to live now?

Second, in what areas of your life—persistent temptations, habitual failings, uncomfortable relationships, even frightening ministry opportunities—do you need to rely more consistently on the resurrection power of Jesus Christ? Pick out one or two and think through practically how the resurrection life you now enjoy can make a difference in how you live.

Third, have you ever been, or are you now, fearful of death—your own or that of a friend or family member? How does the fact that Jesus Christ is the "firstborn from the dead" give you hope when you face this fear? Have you ever thought about what will happen when you die? As for your body, it will cease to function physically and will be buried in the ground. As for you (or your soul or spirit), you will enter immediately into the presence of Jesus in heaven! You will see Him face-to-face and know love, joy, and comfort as never before. Still, you will long for your glorified body. Then, when Jesus returns for a second time to earth, your body that was sloughed off at death will be resurrected and will be reunited with you once again. Then, your salvation will be complete!

He Ascended into Heaven

After appearing throughout the forty days following His resurrection, Jesus ascended into heaven in the sight of His followers. "He led them out as far as Bethany, and He lifted up His hands and blessed them. While He was blessing them, He parted from them" (Luke 24:50–51). Acts 1:9–11 gives more detail: "He was lifted up while they were looking on, and a cloud received Him out of their sight. And as they were gazing intently into the sky while He was going, behold, two men in white clothing stood beside them. They also said, "Men of Galilee, why do you stand looking into the sky? This Jesus, who has been taken up from you into heaven, will come in just the same way as you have watched Him go into heaven" (NASB).

In His last act on this earth, the Son of God, who had descended from heaven to become incarnate as Jesus Christ the God-man, ascended back into heaven. In His glorified body, Jesus was physically removed from this world and His earthly ministry and physically transferred into heaven. Arriving there, "He sat down at the right hand of the Majesty on high" (Heb. 1:3). The ascended Christ will remain there for a time determined by the Father: "Heaven must welcome Him [Jesus] until the times of the restoration of all things" (Acts 3:21). Then He will return a second time, physically descending back to the earth in the same manner that He ascended.

The Significance of Jesus' Ascension

This ascension marked the beginning of new ministries for Jesus: God "raised Him [Christ] from the dead and seated Him at His right hand in the heavenly places, far above all rule and authority and power and dominion, and every name that is named, not only in this age but also in the one to come. And He put all things in subjection under His feet, and gave Him as head over all things to the church, which is His body, the fullness of Him who fills all in all" (Eph. 1:20–23 NASB).

As the "right hand" is the place of authority, Jesus' ascension to the Father's right hand crowned Him with power and sovereignty over every person—every king or queen, president or prime minister—and over every spiritual being—the innumerable angels and seraphim and cherubim and archangels—and over every fallen angel—the hordes of demons and Satan, their ruler—and over the church. Everything—all that exists now and that will ever exist—is subject to our ascended Lord. They can do nothing to us except as God sovereignly and wisely allows them to do so.

Furthermore, the ascension initiated Jesus' eternal ministry of praying for believers: "Christ Jesus is He who died, yes, rather who was raised, who is at the right hand of God, who also intercedes for us" (Rom. 8:34 NASB). He is not inactive, seated at the right hand of the Father. Rather, Jesus "is able also to save forever those who draw near to God through Him, since He always lives to make intercession for them" (Heb. 7:25). He prays for our protection, for our strength to resist temptation, and so forth. He is our advocate, pleading His blood to cover our sins so as to defeat the accuser of His followers, Satan (Rev. 12:10).

Moreover, when He ascended into heaven, Jesus received authority to pour out the Holy Spirit in an unprecedented way upon all those who trust in Him. Jesus Himself promised this to His disciples, who were disturbed by the prophecy that He would soon depart from them: "If you love Me, you will keep My commandments. I will ask the Father, and He will give you another Helper, that He may be with you forever; that is, the Spirit of truth, whom the world cannot receive, because it does not see Him or know Him, but you know Him because He abides with you and will be in you" (John 14:15–17 NASB).

This gift of the Holy Spirit would be especially critical for the kingdom mission on which the disciples would embark: "When the Helper comes, whom I will send to you from the Father, that is, the Spirit of truth who proceeds from the Father, He will testify about Me, and you will testify also, because you have been with Me from the beginning" (John 15:26–27).

Jesus commanded His disciples to wait for the Holy Spirit to come upon them after His ascension. He promised, "You will receive power when the Holy Spirit has come upon you, and you will be My witnesses in Jerusalem, in all Judea and Samaria, and to the ends of the earth" (Acts 1:8). The ascended Jesus would pour out the Holy Spirit upon His disciples, and through His empowering they would launch and carry out their worldwide ministry of proclaiming Christ.

This power to evangelize is only one of the spiritual gifts that would be given by the ascended Christ: "But to each one of us grace was given according to the measure of Christ's gift. Therefore it says, 'When He ascended on high, He led captive a host of captives, and He gave gifts to men" . . . And He [Christ] gave some as apostles, and some as prophets, and some as evangelists, and some as pastors and teachers, for the equipping of the saints for the work of service, to the building up of the body of Christ" (Eph. 4:7-8, 11-12 NASB). Because the ascended Jesus has given spiritual gifts to every believer, the church—the body of Christ—grows and matures and expands.

PAUSE TIME

Consider several issues attached to the ascension. First, how does the ascension of Jesus Christ give you confidence that no person, angel, or demon can exercise any role in your life unless that authority has been approved by Christ Himself?

Sometimes it seems like the world is out of control, completely chaotic, with evil often winning over good. Perhaps you have worried about the power of Satan in your life as well. How does Christ's ascension to the right hand of the Father help you gain a new perspective and overcome your anxieties? How does the fact that Jesus is constantly praying for your protection and strength of character help you to face the very evident evil all around you?

How can you become more dependent on the power of the Holy Spirit as you engage in ministry in your school, church, workplace, and home? Have you ever been fearful when sharing the good news of Jesus Christ because you have serious doubts about being a good witness for Him? Does the promise of the presence of the Holy Spirit as you witness give you encouragement? Also, have you ever thought about which spiritual gift or gifts Christ has given you through the Holy Spirit? How important do you think it is for you to know which gift or gifts you have? Is there someone in your family or church who can help you discern and use your gift(s)?

Jesus' Resurrection and Ascension; Our Resurrection and Ascension

We have already seen the great impact that Jesus' resurrection and ascension have on us as His followers: we enjoy a new resurrection life, we possess an unshakable hope that we too will rise from the dead and live forever with Him, we are the recipients of His intercessory prayers for us, we can be empowered by the Holy Spirit for effective witnessing, and we exercise spiritual gifts to help other Christians grow into Christ-likeness.

All this and more is true because we are identified with Jesus Christ (more about this later). For our purposes, this means that when God considers us in Christ, He considers that we have already been raised with Christ and seated with Christ in heaven: "But God, being rich in mercy, because of His great love with which He loved us, even when we were dead in our transgressions, made us alive together with Christ (by grace you have been saved), and raised us up with Him, and seated us with Him in the heavenly places in Christ Jesus, so that in the ages to come He might show the surpassing riches of His grace in kindness toward us in Christ Jesus" (Eph. 2:4–7 NASB).

Christ was resurrected. In some gracious and mysterious way, we have been resurrected with Him. Christ has ascended and has been seated at the Father's right hand. In some gracious and mysterious way, we have ascended with Him and have been seated with Him in heaven. Such is our identification with Jesus!

This means that our true life now is intimately connected with Jesus: "if you have been raised up with Christ, keep seeking the things above, where Christ is, seated at the right hand of God. Set your mind on the things above, not on the things that are on earth. For you have died and your life is hidden with Christ in God. When Christ, who is our life, is revealed, then you also will be revealed with Him in glory" (Col. 3:1–4 NASB).

Our true identity is tied up with Jesus Christ, so our true life now on earth should not be focused on the things of this world—popularity, the perfect body, clothes and cars, athletic and academic success at the expense of others, and so forth. Rather, our attention should be riveted on the unseen reality that we live with Christ in heaven. This means that we should value the things that Christ valued—truthfulness, faithfulness, obedience, generosity, service to others, mercy, impartiality, integrity—and live the way that Christ lived—following the Word of God, preferring others over our own selves, living in loving relationships characterized by forgiveness and patience, being thankful, depending on God and others, praying constantly, and sharing the good news.

Finally, because we have been resurrected with Christ and seated with Him in the heavens, we never have to be afraid of death. As we look forward to receiving our resurrection bodies and actually living with Christ forever in heaven, we should always recall this affirmation of ultimate victory:

When this perishable [body] will have put on the imperishable, and this mortal will have put on immortality, then will come about the saying that is written, "Death is swallowed up in victory. O death, where is your victory? O death, where is your sting." The sting of death is sin, and the power of sin is the law; but thanks be to God, who gives us the victory through our Lord Jesus Christ. Therefore, my beloved brethren, be steadfast, immovable, always abounding in the work of the Lord, knowing that your toil is not in vain in the Lord. (1 Cor. 15:54–58 NASB)

We have been resurrected and seated with Christ. Though one day we will die physically, we can be assured that when Christ returns, we will receive new glorified bodies and live with Him forever. This is also true of all believers among our family members, our friends, our colleagues at work, our fellow students, and those at our church. Tragedy may strike you or them, and life—physical life, that is—may be cut short, but that is not the end of the story for those who know Jesus Christ personally. Let us never grow weary of telling others about this good news, so that many others may share in our hope and our glorious future.

PAUSE TIME

How can being identified with Jesus Christ's resurrection and ascension help you figure out your own identity in the following contexts?

- As a teenager faced with an identity crisis as you move from childhood to adulthood.
- As a student encountering peer pressure to conform to the expectations and desires of others rather than those of God.

- As a friend to many who have few genuine examples of committed Christians.
- As a son or daughter of parents who are trying to figure out who you really are and how they should raise you.

BRIDGE

Up to this point, I have focused on Jesus Christ and what He did to accomplish our salvation. The deity and humanity of the God-man, His death on the cross as an atoning sacrifice for our sins, the propitiation/reconciliation/redemption that He carried out, His resurrection and ascension—all of this constitutes the work of Christ on our behalf. What an incredible Savior and awesome salvation we have indeed!

I now want to turn from the accomplishment of salvation by Jesus Christ to the application of that salvation to our life. How does our incredible Savior and His awesome salvation become a reality for us personally? Of course, assumed in this question is the recognition that we need a Savior and salvation. This is so, because we are fallen human beings corrupted by sin and guilty because of sin. Though made in God's image, we are not what we should be—the image is marred, tainted, polluted, and defaced by sin. Though created for God's glory, "all have sinned and fall short of the glory of God" (Rom. 3:23).

Instead of offering God our obedience, we are characterized by disobedience. Instead of trusting God and depending on Him, we are characterized by unfaithfulness. Instead of placing our hope in God and His will for us, we are characterized by hopelessness. All of this spells certain doom for us: we are liable to God's judgment, punishment, and condemnation—both in this life and for all eternity. And so we will suffer unimaginable torment and wrath forever—unless God intervenes in our lives.

And so we turn our attention to how the salvation accomplished by Jesus Christ becomes applied to and activated in our lives.

CHAPTER EIGHT

CHOICES IN ETERNITY AND TIME

I 'm not much of an evangelist. Sure, I have shared the good news about Jesus Christ many times and am able to make the gospel clear so that people can understand it. Still, I have not seen many of those people embrace Jesus Christ. Despite this apparent lack of success, I'm glad to tell people about Jesus.

What never ceases to amaze is that, when I communicate the love and forgiveness of Christ, one person (let's call her Jenn) will be interested and may even respond positively to what I'm saying, while another person (let's call him Joe) will yawn and respond negatively. What can account for this difference in responses?

The answer to my question seems obvious and straightforward: Jenn realizes her need for God's love and forgiveness and so believes in Jesus, while Joe prefers his current way of life and continues in his indifference or rebellion toward God. It is Jenn's choice and Joe's choice that accounts for this difference in responses.

Certainly, this is true! I cannot help but wonder, however, if that is only a partial explanation. From my understanding of the Bible, neither Jenn nor Joe is naturally disposed to obey God and do what pleases Him (Eph. 2:1–3). So while I can understand why Joe continues on his normal path—he prefers to go his own way and not God's way—I can't grasp why Jenn moves away from her usual direction and turns toward Christ . . . unless it is God moving in her heart so that she becomes receptive to my words of the gospel. But that seems to be God's decision and not hers, though it certainly doesn't exclude the choice that she makes to believe in Christ.

Does God make a choice for us, and then we make a choice for God?

I further wonder that if this is the case—that God chooses Jenn and she chooses God, and God doesn't choose Joe and Joe doesn't choose God—could Jenn choose not to choose God? And could Joe choose to choose God even though God does not choose him?

Does God's choice of Jenn *determine* her choice of God, or does God just *know* that Jenn will choose Him (so His choice doesn't determine hers)? And does God's decision not to choose Joe *determine* his rejection of Christ, or does God just *know* that Joe will not choose Him (so God's choice doesn't determine Joe's)? (If this sounds like the debate over God's sovereignty and human responsibility and freedom, you are right on target! See chapter 10 of my first *Getting Deep* book on God for further discussion on that topic.)

Questions, questions, questions! But these are not unimportant questions over which we merely speculate and argue.

These questions get at the very heart of how Jenn and Joe—and you and I and our friends and family and fellow students and colleagues at work—experience salvation through Jesus Christ.

As I understand Scripture, two choices are involved, and both are absolutely necessary for people like Jenn and Joe and you and me to embrace Jesus Christ.

The Eternal Choice of God (Election)

Several chapters ago, I asked you to imagine existence before the world came into being. No earth, no sky, no water, no land, no people, no space, no time, no nothingness. Only God—the eternal Father, Son, and Holy Spirit—existed. Love was shared and enjoyed among the three, their radiant glory was splendid, their sense of pleasure with each other was perfect. And purpose existed in the Godhead. Part of that purpose eternally shared between the Father, the Son, and the Holy Spirit was to create a universe consisting of the heavens and the earth and all that they contain. Part of that plan was the creation of human beings—you and me—in the image of God, so that we, like a mirror, would reflect God in the world in which we live. Part of that eternal project was the sending of the Son to earth to give His life for the salvation of fallen human beings: "you were not redeemed with perishable things like silver or gold from your futile way of life inherited from your forefathers, but with precious blood, as of a lamb unblemished and spotless, the blood of Christ. For He was foreknown before the foundation of the world" (1 Pet. 1:18–20 NASB).

Before the world was created, God had purposed as part of His eternal plan that Jesus Christ would be the perfect sacrificial lamb whose blood would be shed to rescue us from our sinfulness. So the death of Jesus Christ for the sins of humanity was not an after-thought with God. Rather, from eternity past, God considered His Son to be the suffering servant. No wonder the early Christians said that Jesus was "delivered up according to God's determined plan and foreknowledge" (Acts 2:23) so that His enemies, in crucifying Christ, fulfilled what God's "plan had predestined to take place" (Acts. 4:28). What God eternally purposed—predestined, ordained, or foreknew—concerning His Son was brought about in the space-time reality of our world when Jesus died on the cross for our sins.

One other aspect of that eternal project of God deserves our attention. Part of that plan includes God's own choice of some human beings to experience His love and forgiveness through Jesus Christ: "Blessed be the God and Father of our Lord Jesus Christ, who has blessed us with every spiritual blessing in the heavens, in Christ; for He chose us in Him, before the foundation of the world, to be holy and blameless in His sight. In love He predestined us to be adopted through Jesus Christ for Himself, according to His favor and will, to the praise of His glorious grace that He favored us with in the Beloved" (Eph. 1:3–6).

Before the world was created, as part of His eternal plan, God chose or predestined us—those who embrace the gospel—in Jesus Christ to belong to Him as His adopted sons and daughters. This is often referred to as *election*. Election was certainly not based on anything we would ever be or would ever do—God's choice of us was not conditioned on our beauty or attractiveness, our intelligence or wisdom, our outstanding efforts or good works.

Speaking of God's gracious choice, the Bible notes that "if by grace, then it is not by works; otherwise grace ceases to be grace" (Rom. 11:6).[17] Indeed, our sin had separated us from God, tearing apart our relationship with Him and rendering us unlovable in ourselves. But His election of us was free, gracious, completely unconditional—it was based only on His sovereign will and good pleasure. God chose us in Christ because He freely desired to do so. It pleased Him to do so—period.

But this wasn't a capricious choice. God did not just randomly pick Jenn but not Joe, or toss you into the "winners" pile and throw one of your best friends into the "losers" pile. Certainly not! God's choice was not a fickle, random selection; rather, it was His gracious choice (we did not God's choice of us) to rescue us from our sin and impending judgment. It was His purposeful choice of Jenn and you and me to pursue us, find us, draw us, and intimately and personally love us forever and ever. God chose us to be His sons and daughters through Jesus Christ!

This should not surprise us because, as we have seen, all that comes to pass is the outworking of the comprehensive, sovereign plan of our mighty God: "we have obtained an inheritance, having been predestined according to His purpose who works all things after the counsel of His will, to the end that we who were the first to hope in Christ would be to the praise of His glory" (Eph. 1:11–12 NASB). Clearly, we who are chosen can offer only one response to this undeserved act of God's love: dedicate our lives entirely to Christ and give all honor and praise to our glorious God and His magnificent grace. Nothing else would be worthy of God's eternal purpose in choosing us to be His children forever.

Election is the eternal choice of God.

Our Choice in Time (Conversion)

What I've said so far might lead to a misunderstanding of the way God works out His gracious choice of us in our life. We might wrongly think that if from all eternity God elected us in Christ for salvation, then at some point in our life He will simply *make* us become followers of Jesus. Our becoming a Christian just automatically takes place—salvation happens—because God determines that it will for us! If that's your understanding, then I need to clarify something.

In one of his letters, Paul writes, "We should always give thanks to God for you, brethren beloved by the Lord, because God has chosen you from the beginning for salvation through sanctification by the Spirit and faith in the truth. It was for this He called you through our gospel, that you may gain the glory of our Lord Jesus Christ" (2 Thess. 2:13–14 NASB).

In thanking God, Paul repeats what we have already seen about election: God has eternally chosen some people to enjoy the experience of salvation. This experience comes about through two important actions. One is the work of the Holy Spirit: sanctification involves our growth in reflecting God and His character and our gradual yet constant separation from sin and its effects. This is God's own activity to bring about salvation in our lives.

The other action is our belief in the truth: Faith involves our willful acceptance of God's invitation to salvation when we hear the good news about Jesus Christ. This is our own human activity to appropriate salvation in our life. Both activities are crucial: God must work, and we must respond to Him.

Notice: God chooses us to experience salvation, and we choose God to experience salvation. Furthermore, God's choice of us by no means minimizes or eliminates our choice of Him. Indeed, we must choose Jesus Christ or we cannot experience salvation. In fact, this response to the gospel is the clear indication that we have been chosen by God for salvation. As Paul expresses his thanks to God in prayer for Christians, he does so "knowing, brethren beloved by God, His choice of you; for our gospel did not come to you in word only, but also in power and in the Holy Spirit and with full conviction; . . . You also became imitators of us and of the Lord, having received the word in much tribulation with the joy of the Holy Spirit" (1 Thess. 1:4–6 NASB). Paul knew these people were chosen by God because they embraced the good news of Jesus Christ.

Conversion Involves Repentance

Let's look more closely at this choice in time, often referred to as conversion. Conversion consists of two activities: repentance from sin and faith in Jesus Christ. As we have seen, the first activity of repentance, or turning from sin, is a key part of the gospel message. As He launched His earthly ministry, Jesus challenged people: "Repent, because the kingdom of heaven has come near!" (Matt. 4:17). Jesus commissioned His disciples to communicate that gospel throughout the entire world, saying, "This is what is written: the Messiah would suffer and rise from the dead the third day, and repentance for forgiveness of sins would be proclaimed in His name to all the nations, beginning at Jerusalem. You are witnesses of these things" (Luke 24:46–48).

In the first Christian sermon ever delivered, Peter urged, "Repent, and each of you be baptized in the name of Jesus Christ for the forgiveness of your sins; and you will receive the gift of the Holy Spirit. For the promise is for you and your children and for all who are far off, as many as the Lord our God will call to Himself" (Acts 2:38–39 NASB). As Paul spoke with the philosophers of Athens, he said, "Having overlooked the times of ignorance, God is now declaring to men that all people everywhere should repent, because He has fixed a day in which He will judge the world in righteousness through a Man whom He has appointed, having furnished proof to all men by raising Him from the dead" (Acts 17:30–31 NASB).

Repentance, or turning from sin, is an essential element of conversion. Specifically, repentance entails three elements (intellectual, emotional, and willful). The first is an intellectual understanding that sin is wrong and deeply grieves and offends God. This involves a change of perspective, for as pre-Christians we once accepted and even excused our sinful behavior, but we now realize the awfulness and harmfulness of sin. The second element is an emotional sorrow for sin. This involves a change of feeling, for as nonbelievers we once enjoyed our sinful passions, but we now sense regret and remorse for our sinfulness. The third is a willful decision to renounce sin and to forsake it. This involves a change of purpose, for as non-Christians we once chose to live in sin, but we now intentionally commit to abandon our sinful living.

All three aspects—intellectual, emotional, willful—are involved in repentance from sin. It is simply not adequate to admit mentally that we have sinned. You probably know people who intellectually agree that they are sinners because the Bible indicates that to be the case, but they are incapable of admitting any specific errors on their part in broken relationships, in family difficulties, in failed jobs. Likewise, it is not enough to feel sorry for our sins. You probably know people who are sorry for their failures, but they merely regret that their problems were exposed and caused punitive damages. For true repentance to take place, a willful decision to turn away from sin must accompany intellectual understanding of, and emotion sorrow for, sin.

I vividly recall grasping these three elements of repentance. I had stolen a sign out of a cornfield and proudly displayed it in my room. Several years later I understood intellectually that my stealing was a sin. I also felt remorse for my wrong action. For true repentance to take place, I had to decide to write a letter to the company that owned the sign. I informed the company of what I had done, asked for forgiveness, and offered to send money as restitution for the cost of the sign. A wonderful letter from the company assured me that my repentance was complete—with intellectual, emotional, and willful elements.

Conversion Involves Faith

The second activity of conversion is faith, or turning to Jesus Christ. This is also referred to as trust. In conversion we cease relying upon ourselves and our own efforts to please God, instead trusting in Christ and Christ alone to bring us into a relationship with God. Jesus Himself emphasized this aspect of belief: "For God so loved the world that He gave His only begotten Son, that whoever believes in Him shall not perish, but have eternal life" (John 3:16).

When a suicidal Philippian jailor asked the apostles what he could do to be saved, they responded, "Believe on the Lord Jesus, and you will be saved—you and your household" (Acts 16:31). Because salvation is solely by God's grace, the only possible response that we can offer to accept this gift is faith: "For by grace you are saved through faith, and this is not from yourselves; it is God's gift—not from works, so that no one can boast" (Eph. 2:8-9). Faith, or turning to Jesus Christ, is an essential element of conversion, our choice of salvation when we hear the good news of Jesus Christ.

Faith involves the same three elements as repentance (intellectual, emotional, and willful). Faith requires an intellectual understanding of who Jesus is and what He has done to accomplish salvation for us. The basics of the gospel must be grasped. As Paul explained: "'Whoever will call on the name of the Lord will be saved.' How then will they call on Him in whom they have not believed? How will they believe in Him whom they have not heard? And how will they hear without a preacher? How will they preach unless they are sent?" (Rom. 10:13–15 NASB). This need for people to understand the gospel is a key reason for communicating the good news about Jesus Christ.

Faith also requires an emotional sense that the gospel resolves our problem of sin and meets the deepest needs of our lives. We must approve the message of salvation as being specifically directed to our lives. And faith requires a willful decision to trust in Jesus Christ to save us from sin. This involves definitively forsaking whatever we formerly relied upon to make us acceptable to God—our being raised in a Christian home, our religious activities, our good works to help others, our ability to figure it all out—and depending on Christ and Christ alone.

All three aspects—intellectual, emotional, willful—are involved in turning to Jesus Christ in faith. It is simply not adequate to be able to recount the facts about Jesus. You probably know people who intellectually can recite plenty of things about Jesus, but those facts make no difference at all in their life. Likewise, it is not enough to get emotionally worked up about Jesus when we worship Him or when we face deep problems that we are unable to handle. For genuine faith to be expressed, a willful decision to trust Jesus Christ for salvation must accompany intellectual understanding and emotional approval of the gospel.

When I trusted Christ for my salvation, I intellectually understood the truths of the gospel. I also had a deep, almost overpowering sense of my need for Christ to rescue me. By crying out to God to save me, I willfully decided to trust Christ to do just that. The change that took place in my life assured me that my faith was genuine—with intellectual, emotional, and willful elements.

Because this second activity in conversion—faith—is commonly misunderstood today, I want to explain a bit more about it. The misunderstanding revolves around the term we use to describe it. Unless we explain it, the term *faith* often communicates that salvation in Jesus Christ involves an irrational commitment—a so-called leap of faith. That is, supposedly in spite of strong evidence to the contrary—Jesus Christ did not really exist, did not really teach what the Bible says He taught or do the things the Bible says He did—we believe that He did anyway. That is not what we mean by faith!

Similarly, the term *belief* or *believe* often communicates an intellectual assent to Jesus with no personal commitment to or dependence upon him. Indeed, many people of other religions—Muslims, Hindus, Buddhists—believe that Jesus lived, taught great wisdom, and healed people, but such belief does not make them Christians (since they believe that He was only a prophet or teacher and not the Son of God who rose from the dead to be a sacrifice for our sins). As we have seen, faith is our human response to the good news of Jesus Christ, and it entails intellectual, emotional, and willful elements.

Conversion Involves Both Repentance and Faith

So conversion consists of two activities: repentance from sin and faith in Jesus Christ. In the Old Testament, these two activities are linked in an appeal to all humanity:

Seek the LORD while He may be found;
Call upon Him while He is near.
Let the wicked forsake his way
And the unrighteous man his thoughts;
And let him return to the LORD,
And He will have compassion on him,
And to our God,
For He will abundantly pardon. (Isa. 55:6–7 NASB)

To experience salvation, the wicked or unrighteous man must forsake his evil doing and thinking (repentance from sin) and return to the Lord (faith).

Conversion is our choice in time.

The Divine and Human Choices

So two choices are involved in the matter of salvation: God chooses us to experience salvation, and we choose God to experience salvation. God's choice of us takes place outside of time; indeed, His choice was made from eternity past, before human beings whom He chose to experience salvation even existed. Our choice of God takes place when, in repentance and faith, we turn from sin and embrace Jesus Christ through the gospel. Furthermore, God's choice of us by no means minimizes or eliminates our choice of Him. Indeed, we must choose Jesus Christ or we cannot experience salvation.

Is it possible for us to understand more fully how these two choices coincide or work together? Yes, but what I'm about to say employs some advanced philosophical thinking, so my answer won't be easy to follow. But let's try it anyway by pulling in our friends Jenn and Joe to help us.

Let's make a distinction between two concepts: necessity and constraint. There are two types of necessity: Necessity type 1 refers to anything that must take place. Anything that God plans to take place will indeed take place, according to the first type of necessity. Indeed, it must take place because God has purposed it will. For example, because God purposed to create human beings in His image (Gen. 1:26), human beings are created in His image (Gen. 1:27). No one or thing can thwart the sovereign will of God, "who works out everything in agreement with the decision of His will" (Eph. 1:11). This is necessity type 1.

Necessity type 2 refers to the fact that any decision or action must take place according to the will and nature of the one who makes the choice or engages in the action. A friend sees you in the hallway at school and tells you to come over. There is no necessity for you to respond to your friend and go over; that is, necessity type 1 does not come into play. But if you decide to respond, there are various ways you can choose to approach your friend. You can walk, run, hop, skip, crawl, somersault, jump, or leap over to your friend. But you can't fly. You must decide and act according to your own will and nature (as a human being), and you can't decide and act according to the will and nature of a bird. You are a human being, and you must decide and act according to your human will and nature. This is necessity type 2.

Let's consider how necessity type 1 and necessity type 2 worked together in the death of Jesus Christ. The crucifixion took place according to necessity type 1 because for all eternity the Father had planned that His Son would die for the sins of the world. But the crucifixion also took place according to necessity type 2. That is, Jesus willingly sacrificed His life and died on the cross. His very existence was committed to fulfilling the Father's role for Him. As Jesus Himself indicated: "This is why the Father loves Me, because I am laying down My life so I may take it up again. No one takes it from Me, but I lay it down on My own" (John 10:17–18). Thus, the crucifixion took place according to the will and nature of Jesus Christ; this is necessity type 2.

Notice that both types of necessity were involved in the death of Jesus Christ. The crucifixion had to take place because the Father had purposed that it would (necessity type 1), and it took place because Jesus Christ decided and acted in accordance to His own will and nature that it would (necessity type 2).

Constraint, like necessity, is also of two types: (1) something takes place without freedom of choice though a willful choice is made and (2) something takes place without freedom of choice and no willful choice is made. Here's an example of constraint type 1: A bank robber comes up to a teller, thrusts a note demanding money into her hand, points a gun at her head, and orders her to put the money into a sack. The teller does not have freedom of choice (she knows she will be killed if she disobeys the thief's instructions). She makes a willful choice to go into the safe, takes some money and places it into the bag, returns to the robber and gives him the money. The teller was under constraint—she did not have freedom of choice—but she did make a willful choice to act. This is constraint of the first type.

Here's an example of constraint type 2: A bike rider hugging the curb as he peddles in the street is hit by an automobile, is propelled fifty feet through the air, and lands with a thud. The bike rider does not have freedom of choice (the car forced him to fly like a projectile through the air) and he does not make a willful choice (he did not choose to be displaced by the car). The bike rider was under constraint—he did not have freedom of choice—and he did not make a willful choice to act. This is constraint of the second type.

Let's apply these concepts of necessity and constraint to our discussion of Jenn and Joe. I want you to think in terms of necessity, not constraint. God's choice of Jenn to experience salvation means that Jenn must experience salvation. Because of God's choice of Jenn, her salvation must take place. This is necessity type 1. At the same time, Jenn's choice of God means that her choice comes about according to Jenn's own will and nature. In other words, Jenn genuinely and truly chooses God because she wants to do so. This is necessity type 2. With this understanding of necessity, we see how God's choice of Jenn makes her choice of Him a necessity (type 1) and how Jenn's choice of God makes her choice of Him a necessity (type 2).

But how about Joe and his choice not to choose God? God's decision not to choose Joe means that Joe will not experience salvation. Because of God's choice to pass over Joe, his salvation will not take place. This is necessity type 1. At the same time, Joe's decision not to choose God means that his choice comes about according to Joe's own will and nature. In other words, Joe genuinely and truly decides not to choose God because he does not want to do so. This is necessity type 2.

Notice: At no point in our discussion does the concept of constraint appear. God's choice of Jenn does not involve constraint. It does not force Jenn against her will to choose God. On the contrary, Jenn chooses God in accordance with her own will and nature. She truly desires to repent of her sin and embrace Jesus Christ by faith, and so she exercises her will to do so. She experiences salvation. Also, God's choice to pass over Joe does not involve constraint. It does not force Joe against his will not to choose God. On the contrary, Joe decides not to choose God in accordance with his own will and nature, and so he exercises his will not to do so. Joe truly prefers his current way of life and continues in his indifference or rebellion toward God.

God chooses Jenn, and so she chooses God. God does not choose Joe, and so he does not choose God. So God's choice determines Jenn's choice and Joe's choice. Be careful, however: Though God's choice determines Jenn's choice, it does so without constraint. Jenn genuinely repents of her sin and expresses faith in Jesus Christ. Her conversion is something she truly desires and chooses. So Jenn could not choose not to choose God. God's choice of Jenn guarantees that she will choose Him, and she genuinely wants to choose Him. Furthermore, though God's not choosing Joe determines his choice, it does so without constraint. Joe genuinely rejects the gospel of Jesus Christ. His refusal to repent and turn to Jesus Christ is something he truly desires and chooses. So Joe could not choose to choose God. God's choice to pass over Joe guarantees that Joe will not choose Him, and Joe genuinely does not want to choose God.

But how does this come about? I think that the Bible gives some insight into how all this happens. From eternity past, God chose Jenn to experience salvation. Yet, because of her sin, she is not naturally disposed to obey God and do what pleases Him. So a "conspiracy of circumstances" is needed to reverse her situation. As Jenn listens to the gospel about Jesus Christ, God draws her to Himself. This is absolutely necessary, because Jesus told us "no one can come to Me unless the Father who sent Me draws him" (John 6:44). The Holy Spirit also impresses upon Jenn the error of her sin, the hopelessness of her self-righteousness, and the futility of her worldly judgment (John 16:8–11).

Also, people pray for Jenn, love Jenn, and show by their life a different way of living. Jenn becomes dissatisfied with her current situation. She becomes sick and tired of her indifference or rebellion toward God. So she embraces the good news of salvation. She turns from her sin and places her faith in Jesus Christ. Jenn's choice is in accordance with her own will and nature, and it is in accordance with God's eternal choice of her.

Like Jenn, Joe is not naturally disposed to obey God and do what pleases Him. So a "conspiracy of circumstances" is not needed to reverse his situation. God simply allows Joe's sinful nature to run its own course. As Joe listens to the gospel about Jesus Christ, God does not draw Joe to Himself. Though the Holy Spirit impresses upon Joe the error of his sin, the hopelessness of his self-righteousness, and the futility of his worldly judgment (John 16:8–11), Joe prefers his current situation. Though people pray for Joe, love Joe, and show by their way of life a different way of living, Joe rejects what they offer. He continues in his indifference or rebellion toward God. When he hears the gospel, he does not respond with repentance and faith, but rejects the good news. Joe's choice is in accordance with his own will and nature, and it is in accordance with God's eternal choice to pass him over.

But isn't this incredibly unfair? Why doesn't God choose both Jenn and Joe to experience salvation? Certainly, God could choose to do this. But we know from both the Bible and our own experience that God does not choose everyone for salvation (if He did, then everyone would experience salvation; but we know this not to be the case). If God could choose to do this, why doesn't He do so?

Here's my best answer to this very tough question: I don't know very much.

I know that the only reason God chooses Jenn for salvation is because this pleases Him. His election of her is unconditional: it is not based on anything she would ever be or would ever do—His choice was not conditioned on her beauty, intelligence, outstanding efforts, or good works. Indeed, I know that Jenn's sin had separated her from God, torn apart her relationship with Him, and rendered her unlovable in herself. No, God's choice of Jenn was gracious, completely unconditional—it was based only on His sovereign will and good pleasure. I also know that God's choice should lead Jenn to dedicate her life entirely to Christ and to praise and thank God for all eternity for His gracious, marvelous work in her life.

I also know that God's decision to pass over Joe was a sorrowful choice. God Himself says, "I take no pleasure in the death of the wicked, but rather that the wicked turn from his way and live" (Ezek. 33:11). It does not delight God that Joe chooses to continue in his indifference or rebellion toward Him. On the contrary, God is "not wanting any to perish, but all to come to repentance" (2 Pet. 3:9). Based on this, we can only reason that God's eternal choice not to choose Joe was a sorrowful choice. And yet God made that choice. Furthermore, I know this choice means that God will demonstrate His justice and wrath against Joe—and He will do so rightly, because Joe's choice not to choose God brings judgment and condemnation on Joe. I know that God is not to blame.

Beyond this, I don't know. And I can't complain and raise objections to God about it either. Indeed, on this issue, God urges me to put my finger over my lips and to remain silent:

But who are you—anyone who talks back to God?
Will what is formed say to the one who formed it, "Why did you make me like this?" Or has the potter no right

over His clay, to make from the same lump one piece of pottery for honor and another for dishonor? And what if God, desiring to display His wrath and to make His power known, endured with much patience objects of wrath ready for destruction? And [what if] He did this to make known the riches of His glory on objects of mercy that He prepared beforehand for glory—on us whom He also called, not only from the Jews but also from the Gentiles? (Rom. 9:20–24)

I am not the potter—God is. He may make of His human creation what He wills. He has the right as the potter to make Jenn for honor and Joe for dishonor. He has the right as the potter to display His wrath and judgment power against Joe as one of the "objects of wrath ready for destruction." And God has the right as the potter to display His grace in the life of Jenn as one of the "objects of mercy that He prepared beforehand for glory."

God has the right to do what He wants.

It is His prerogative—He wills what He wills.

End of story.

But, but, but . . .

End of story.

PAUSE TIME

If your mind is like mine, it is racing with many unanswered questions. I'd love to talk more about this matter with you, but for the time being, put aside those unanswered questions to concentrate on some other important questions.

First, how do you know that God eternally chose you to experience salvation? If you don't know the answer to this question, make sure to review the section on the eternal choice of God at the beginning of this chapter.

Second, on what basis did God make His choice of you? Was His choice conditioned on something in you or on something that you do? Or was His choice unconditional, based solely on His good pleasure and sovereign will to love you? Was His choice of you random and fickle? Or did God choose you personally? How do your answers to these questions affect your response to God's choice of you? Are you giving Him an adequate response to His choice of you, or do you need some work in this area?

Third, did God's choice of you minimize or eliminate your choice of Him? What "conspiracy of circumstances" was involved

in bringing you to this choice? When you embraced Jesus Christ
for salvation, were you constrained to do so, forced against
your will? Or did you choose God in accordance with your own
will and nature? Did you want to choose God? Also, did your
conversion involve both repentance from sin and faith in Jesus
Christ? When you sin now, do you continue to repent of your
sin? Are you continuing to trust Jesus Christ day by day?

Fourth, do you think that God's choice of people to experience salvation is incredibly unfair? Can you think of other
reasons why God decided to pass over some people for salvation?
Is there any way for you to tell ahead of time (that is, before
sharing the gospel with them) those people whom God has elected
and those whom He has not? How does your answer to this question affect your evangelism? How does Paul's discussion in
Romans 9:20-24 (quoted above) affect your thinking about this
issue?

Finally, how can God's eternal choice of you to experience
salvation give you the assurance of salvation—that you truly belong to Him and will for all eternity?

CHAPTER NINE

NEW REALITY, NEW RELATIONSHIP, NEW FAMILY, NEW IDENTITY

I can remember my conversion to Christ like it was only yesterday. I was a senior in high school, and a group of high school students came to our church one fall weekend to tell us about their personal relationship with God. Though I had been raised going to church and had always believed in God, I had never heard of a personal relationship with Him. As soon as I met these fellow students, however, I clearly detected a huge difference between them and me. I concluded there must be something to this "personal relationship" with God.

At a critical moment during that weekend, I asked my new friends to talk about the difference between them and me. As they described it, I was a good, moral, religious kid who was trying hard to earn God's favor and love by doing good things for Him and for others. They, on the other hand, enjoyed a personal relationship with God through Jesus Christ. That is, they had realized that there was nothing they could ever do to merit God's love and friendship. They had turned to God from their sins and embraced Jesus Christ by faith alone, not by their personal efforts. Through this, they had received forgiveness and entered into a personal relationship with God in which He loved them and they loved Him.

I was a bit frustrated at first with their explanation. I couldn't grasp the difference between trying hard to please God and trusting

Jesus Christ to please God for me so I could enjoy a relationship with Him. And I wrestled with my need for forgiveness. After all, I was a very moral kid—quite unlike my new friends were before they had this personal relationship with God.

This difference was particularly pronounced between my life and that of Zeke, one of our guests. Zeke had been a heroin addict. One night after a terrible drug overdose, he entered his home and found his brother asleep on the couch in the living room. In a fit of drug-induced madness, Zeke had gone into the kitchen, pulled out a butcher knife from the drawer, returned to the living room, stood over his brother, and lifted the butcher knife over his head, ready to murder him. Strangely, mysteriously, Zeke dropped the knife, fled from his house into the night, and ended up in a pastor's home. As the pastor shared the good news with Zeke, he embraced Jesus Christ and found forgiveness and a transformed life free from drugs.

But, I objected (to myself and to God, not to others), I was better than Zeke—I was a moral, religious kid! I could see that Zeke needed Jesus, but what did Jesus have to do with me?

Then, suddenly, it clicked. It began with the discovery that in reality, I was no better than Zeke when he had considered cutting off his brother's head. My pursuit after good works to earn God's favor had brought about pride, a sense that I was superior to others—and that was desperately offensive to God. So even if I was moral and religious—in fact, because I was this way—I was as much in need of Jesus Christ as Zeke had been. With this realization of my need, I cried out to Jesus to save me.

Immediately, I knew what a personal relationship with God meant. I had just experienced the first step of it for myself! I felt like a heavy weight had been lifted from my shoulders. I couldn't wait to tell my friends what had just happened. I knew that I had eternal life and that I would live with God forever.

These were my initial experiences as my new relationship with God through Jesus Christ unfolded. Little did I know that what I sensed was only a small bit of all that God had already worked in my life and would continue to develop over the course of time.

A New Creation

The Bible offers a brief summary about what happens when we turn from sin and embrace Jesus Christ by faith: "if anyone is in Christ, there is a new creation; old things have passed away, and look, new things have come" (2 Cor. 5:17). Everything that was formerly true of us—our shame, our sense of feeling dirty, our weight of guilt, our alienation, our dreaded fears, our lostness, our hopelessness, our indifference, our rebellion, our unbelief—no longer exists. The slate is wiped clean. The files are deleted; the records are destroyed. The past that once haunted us is gone.

In the place of our sinful reality, a brand-new reality is launched. We become new people—totally, decisively, and irrevocably new. In the Bible, this newness of life is described in all its awesome fullness: we are born again, we are declared not guilty but righteous instead, we join a new family, and we gain a new identity.

The New Reality (Regeneration)

Perhaps you've heard the term *born again:* "You must be born again!" "I'm a born-again Christian." This expression comes from a story about Jesus and Nicodemus, who was a high-ranking religious leader and secret follower of Jesus:

> Now there was a man of the Pharisees, named Nicodemus, a ruler of the Jews; this man came to Jesus by night and said to Him, "Rabbi, we know that You have come from God as a teacher; for no one can do these signs that You do unless God is with him." Jesus answered and said to him, "Truly, truly, I say to you, unless one is born again he cannot see the kingdom of God." Nicodemus said to Him, "How can a man be born when he is old? He cannot enter a second time into his mother's womb and be born, can he?" Jesus answered, "Truly, truly, I say to you, unless one is born of water and the Spirit he cannot enter into the kingdom of God." That which is born of the flesh is flesh, and that which is born of the Spirit is spirit. Do not be amazed that I said to you, 'You must be born again.' The wind blows where it wishes and you hear the sound of it, but do not know

where it comes from and whence it is going; so is everyone who is born of the Spirit." (John 3:1-8 NASB)

According to Jesus, one thing is essential for entering into a
relationship with God in which He reigns and rules: a new birth.
Quite humorously, Nicodemus completely missed the point, believing that Jesus meant that he, grown-up Nicodemus, needed
to be reborn physically. (Undoubtedly, Nicodemus' mother would
recoil from that idea—once was more than enough for her!)

But Jesus did not refer to a physical birth; after all, Nicodemus
already possessed biological life. Rather, Jesus was talking about a
spiritual birth—a new life that comes from above, from God. This
rebirth comes about through the cleansing forgiveness of sin and
indwelling presence of the Holy Spirit.[18] While living in the realm
of the flesh, as physically born of his parents' biological material,
Nicodemus would begin living a new spiritual reality as born again
of the Holy Spirit.

And so it is true of all who experience the new birth: We enter
into a new reality, a new life in the Spirit of God. As Jesus Himself
indicated, this is quite mysterious. We cannot see and control the
wind, but we detect its presence and power by hearing its sound and
observing the bended trees and the leaves that are whipped here
and there by it. In the same way, we cannot grasp and control the
Holy Spirit. But we can observe the presence and power of the Spirit
through the new birth as experienced by the followers of Jesus.

All who are born again live a new reality. The old reality, dom-
inated by concerns of material existence and life in this world,
is canceled. What once loomed large in stress-producing importance—popularity, security, clothes and cars, comfort, indepen-
dence, power, material success, athletic and academic accomplishment at all costs—begins to fade away. In its place, God and His
priorities—purity, integrity, faithfulness, love, dependence, forgiveness, patience, worship, thankfulness, service—begin to reign increasingly supreme.

This new birth is also called regeneration, emphasizing the de-
liverance from spiritual death. As the Bible affirms, we are "dead
in [our] trespasses and sins" (Eph. 2:1) before the new birth takes
place. Clearly, we are in need of moral and spiritual transformation, or regeneration. As we have seen, this takes place by the Holy

Spirit. Indeed, God plays the sole role in our regeneration; we can contribute nothing at all to being born again: "But to all who did receive Him, He gave them the right to be children of God, to those who believe in His name, who were born, not of blood, or of the will of the flesh, or of the will of man, but of God" (John 1:12–13).

This regeneration involves the hearing of the Word of God:
You have been born again—not of perishable seed
but of imperishable—through the living and enduring word of God. For
    All flesh is like grass,
    and all its glory like a flower of the grass.
The grass withers, and the flower drops off,
but the word of the Lord endures forever.
And this is the word that was preached as the gospel
to you. (1 Pet. 1:23–25)

When we hear the gospel of Jesus Christ communicated, God uses His Word to bring about the new birth in our lives. Again, the Bible affirms: "By His own choice, He gave us a new birth by the message of truth" (James 1:18). Regeneration, or the new birth, then, is not a decision or action on our part, but is the work of God the Holy Spirit through His Word. Regeneration removes us from spiritual death and imparts to us new spiritual life.

How can we tell if we have experienced the new birth? Sometimes Christians erect a checklist of dos and don'ts that is supposed to give definitive indications of whether someone has truly been born again. Some of the dos include going to church several times a week, reading the Bible, praying, telling others about Jesus, etc. The don'ts supposedly include refraining from smoking, gambling, using drugs, drinking alcoholic beverages, going to movies, dancing, engaging in pre- or extramarital sex, etc. Unfortunately, many of these checklists emphasize external changes that may be easily measurable but may not be true indicators of the new birth.

Scripture itself indicates that certain realities accompany regeneration. These include a growing practice of righteousness (1 John 2:29), a progressive freedom from persistent sin (1 John 3:9), the development of authentic love for others (1 John 4:7), increasing power to resist temptations toward sin and pressures to revert to our old way of life (1 John 5:3–4), and protection from the wicked attacks and deceptive challenges of the evil one (1 John 5:18). If we would rely on these biblical indicators of the new birth, we would be more conscious of what Jesus wants to develop in His followers and would avoid erecting illegitimate standards that are very often powerless to bring about the changes desired by the Holy Spirit.

PAUSE TIME

Did you have a dramatic experience of regeneration? Or did you experience this work of God in a more quiet, unassuming way? What biblical indicators of regeneration have you seen in your life that clearly show you are born again?

The New Relationship (Justification)

Not only does God work powerfully to impart new spiritual life to us, transforming our nature through the new birth, He also works to establish a new relationship with us. To grasp this reality, think of God as our judge. (As Genesis 18:25 notes, God is "the Judge of all the earth.") Imagine appearing before God in a courtroom. He is the judge to whom you must give an account of everything you have ever done. Right or wrong. Out in the open or hidden. Thoughts, attitudes, motivations. Actions, words, goals. Things done, things left undone. Imagine giving an explanation for your thoughts and activities to God the judge.

If you are like me, such a scenario—even an imagined scenario—scares me to death. Could I imagine anything other than a grade of F, a judgment of total failure? Could I hope for any verdict other than guilty? Could you? I could not, if I'm honest with myself. My sin renders me guilty and liable to condemnation before God. Isn't the same true of you?

Now, imagine a new scene. God, the judge of all the earth, declares you and me not guilty but righteous. Total fiction, no doubt! How could God ever consider us in this way? Remember, as the judge of all the earth, "all His ways are entirely just" (Deut. 32:4). God does not treat the wicked and the righteous alike (Gen. 18:25); indeed, as Isaiah the prophet announced:

> Tell the righteous that it will go well [for them],
> for they will eat the fruit of their deeds.

> Woe to the wicked—[it will go] badly [for them],
> for what they have done will be done to them.
> (Isa. 3:10–11)

How can we, who are sinful and deserve nothing other than God's condemnation, expect that it will go well for us, as only the righteous deserve?

In what has been called the "sweet exchange," God substitutes our sin for Christ's righteousness. All of our sins, together with the guilt and condemnation deserved because of our sins, are transferred to Jesus Christ. Dying on the cross, He bore our guilt and condemnation, paying the price for our sins in our place. This is called the imputation of sin to Christ.

At the same time, the righteousness of Jesus Christ—remember, He perfectly obeyed the Father in everything and never once sinned—is transferred to us. This is called the imputation of Christ's righteousness to us. Just as when we deposit a check from a friend or employer into our bank, and the money is credited to our personal account, so God credits the righteousness of His Son into our account. Then, when He views us, He no longer considers us as guilty but as righteous instead. Our sin has been exchanged for the righteousness of Jesus Christ.

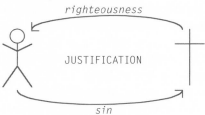

This work of God to establish a new relationship with us is called justification. Go back to the courtroom scene: God as the judge justifies us; that is, He bangs down His gavel and declares us not guilty but righteous instead. This is what Paul emphasizes in Romans 3:26: "He presented Him to demonstrate His righteousness at the present time, so that He would be righteous and declare righteous the one who has faith in Jesus." God Himself is just in making this legal declaration because Jesus has truly paid the penalty for our sins and His righteousness is truly credited to our account.

Notice that God does not just pretend to deal with sin; He does not ignore our problem, nor does He brush aside sin without taking care of it. Rather, God remains just because He punishes sin (though the punishment is exacted from Jesus Christ) and justifies us by declaring us not guilty but righteous instead.

Clearly, justification is a gift, not something we could ever earn or achieve by our own merits. Paul affirms this: "all have sinned and fall short of the glory of God. They are justified freely by His grace through the redemption that is in Christ Jesus" (Rom. 3:23-24). The ground or basis of our justification is the salvation that Jesus Christ accomplished for us through His perfect life and sacrificial death for our sins. The only response that we can offer to God is to receive this gift; that is, our only response is faith. As we saw above, God is righteous and declares "righteous the one who has faith in Jesus" (Rom. 3:26). Justification is by faith, and faith alone; we cannot be justified by doing good works. Again, Paul emphasizes this: "For we conclude that a man is justified by faith apart from works of law" (Rom. 3:28).

But certainly there is something that we can do—give money to the poor, provide food and blankets for the homeless, help a struggling student with math homework, volunteer for some good cause—that will release us from part of our sin and earn a small bit of righteousness for our account, isn't there? Nice try, even admirable in terms of helping others! But all of our attempts to earn justification fall far short of achieving forgiveness for our sins and acquiring righteousness before God.

Just to make sure we don't miss this point, Paul repeats it over and over again: "knowing that a man is not justified by the works of the Law but through faith in Christ Jesus, even we have believed in Christ Jesus, so that we may be justified by faith in Christ and not by the works of the Law; since by the works of the Law no flesh will be justified" (Gal. 2:16 NASB). Faith, not our good works, is the means by which we receive God's justification. He does not justify those who try hard to earn His love and forgiveness.

In fact, Paul notes: "to the one who does not work, but believes in Him who justifies the ungodly, his faith is credited as righteousness" (Rom. 4:5 NASB). God reserves His justification for the ungodly who seek Him—for those who have given up attempting to make themselves better to win God over to their side. When we cease trying to do good works to earn God's favor, then we can be justified—declared not guilty but righteous instead—by faith.

Justification is crucially important for our lives. Paul explains that "having been justified by faith, we have peace with God through our Lord Jesus Christ" (Rom. 5:1 NASB). This peace is far more than a temporary feeling that is strengthened or weakened by the good or bad circumstances of our lives. Rather, it is the reality that we are no longer separated from God because of our indifference and rebellion. Our new reality of peace means that we fully enjoy His forgiveness and love—we now experience a personal, intimate, living relationship with God Himself!

PAUSE TIME

Are you glad that God justifies the ungodly? Why? Why should you be thankful for God's imputation of your sins to Jesus Christ and His righteousness to you?

If you were someone who worked very hard to earn God's favor, yet could not know for sure if you had been good enough for God to justify you, what would this truth of imputation mean for your assurance (or lack of assurance) of salvation? As a follower of Jesus Christ whom God now views as being completely righteous, do you ever need to fear facing God as your judge?

The New Family (Adoption)

What more could we hope for than this? But God is not done yet in our experience of salvation. As if a new birth and a new relationship with Him were not enough, God also makes us members of a new family. This work of God is called adoption. Adoption encompasses several elements. First, we are "children of God" (John 1:12) who relate to Him as our Father. Before embracing Jesus Christ, we were slaves of our indifference and rebellion toward God; we did not know God personally as Father. Now, however, we have received "adoption as sons. And because you are sons, God has sent the Spirit of His Son into our hearts, crying, 'Abba, Father!' So you are no longer a slave, but a son" (Gal. 4:5-7).

As adopted children of God, we relate to Him intimately as our Father. With terms of endearment (like "Dad" or "Daddy"), we talk with Him and trust Him to do right by us always. We rely on Him as Father to provide for all our needs—wise guidance for our life, strength to obey Him when the going gets tough, and comfort when we are hurt and disturbed by life's unfair circumstances. We tell our Father that we love Him, and we thank Him for His work in our lives. Ever mindful not to disappoint or sadden Him, we seek to please Him in all that we are and do. We imitate Him, reflecting His character in the world in which we live (Eph. 5:1; 1 Pet. 1:14–16). As His beloved children, we enjoy nothing more than being with our Father, just as He desires an intimate relationship with us.

The second element of our adoption as children of God is that we belong to the family composed of all followers of Jesus Christ. Together, we are all brothers and sisters, members of the family of God. Whatever else of note that divides or distinguishes us—skin color, language, economic or social status, gender, style of clothes, intellectual or athletic abilities, body type, and so forth—ultimately fade away in light of the commonalities that we possess in Jesus Christ: "There is one body and one Spirit, just as you were called to one hope at your calling; one Lord, one faith, one baptism, one God and Father of all, who is above all and through all and in all" (Eph. 4:4–6).

Perhaps like me, you have had the privilege of meeting Christians from other parts of the world, either through a foreign-exchange program at school or participation in a short-term missions project through church. Even in the first encounter, a common bond—a sense of connection—joins you and them, even if you speak different languages, come from different churches, worship God in different ways, have different appearances, and live very different lifestyles. We realize there is far more that unites us than divides us because we have been adopted as brothers and sisters into the same family with the same Father, Lord, and Holy Spirit.

This reality is especially important for those who come from dysfunctional families in which relationships with parents and siblings were broken or even nonexistent, in which acceptance was conditioned on being beautiful or smart or athletic or successful, in which harmony more often than not gave way to bitter conflict, and in which love was extended or withheld randomly—when it was present, love was chaotic rather than continuous.

PAUSE TIME

When you think of relating to God as your Father, how does the relationship (or lack of it) you had/have with your bio-logical father or stepfather affect your relationship with your Father? Are there some negative experiences with your own father (betrayal, abandonment, unreasonable discipline, verbal/emotional/physical abuse, unfaithfulness to your mother, favoritism of you or your siblings) that negatively impact your relationship with God?

Is there a pastor or youth worker or friend with whom you could talk about these things? Are there some positive experi-ences with your own father (sense of protection, provision of your needs and those of your family, positive reinforcement of right attitudes and actions, clear demonstrations of love) that you can recall and intensify so that they positively impact your relationship with God?

What does it mean for you that the Christians around you—your friends, fellow students at school, colleagues at work, members of your youth group and church—are your brothers and sisters? Does this indicate something of how you should treat them and relate to them? Do you know some Christians who are difficult to relate to? How does the reality that they are your brothers and sisters in Christ help you relate to them?

The New Identity (Being "in Christ")

In the previous section, we saw that the Bible indicates that as Christians, we are all part of "one body" (Eph. 4:4). This image, like that of a family, speaks of our connectedness with Jesus Christ and one another. This is due to being given a new identity when we embrace Christ. As the Bible explains: "For even as the body is one and yet has many members, and all the members of the body, though they are many, are one body, so also is Christ. For by one Spirit we were all baptized into one body, whether Jews or Greeks, whether slaves or free, and we were all made to drink of one Spirit" (1 Cor. 12:12–13 NASB).

Look at this picture of the church: Jesus Christ is the head of the body, and we as individuals compose the various mem-bers—eyes, feet, hands, ears—of that one body. Yes, we are many, and we are very different from one another; yet, there is only one body—the body of Christ. Membership in this body takes place when Christ Himself baptizes us with the Holy Spirit into His body. This baptism is not a physical reality, like our baptism with water. Rather, it is a spiritual reality that identifies us with Christ and with one another. As members of the same body, we belong to Him and to one another.

The Bible also refers to this reality as being "in Christ." As human beings descended from the same original parents, all of us share an identity of being "in Adam." In terms of our origin, we all can trace our roots to Adam and Eve. As created beings, we all share certain characteristics that distinguish us from other creatures—we are embodied beings who are different from angels, animals, plants, and so forth.

Moreover, we are beings created in the image of God, meaning that we are designed like mirrors to reflect God in the world in which we live. Tragically, because our first parents sinned and their fall exerted a terrible impact on all their descendants, we are infected with sin, thoroughly corrupted in nature, guilty before God, and liable to eternal punishment. All of this constitutes our identity "in Adam."

When we embrace Jesus Christ by faith, we are given a new identity. Though still human, still descended from our original parents, still image bearers of God, and still sinners, we have a new primary identity—we are "in Christ": a status that claims several key considerations. As we have seen, it means that we have been chosen by God for salvation. Remember what the Bible notes about this: God "chose us in Him [Christ] before the foundation of the world" (Eph. 1:4). It also means that we have been given grace for salvation. As the Bible further explains: God "saved us and called us with a holy calling, not according to our works, but according to His own purpose and grace, which was given to us in Christ Jesus before time began (2 Tim. 1:9). Before we were born, even before the world was created, God determined that we would enjoy a special relationship with Him, and this election was carried out "in Christ."

Furthermore, being "in Christ" means that we are identified with the key events in the life of Jesus. So when God considers us as being "in Christ," He counts that we have experienced what Christ Himself experienced. Specifically, we are identified with Christ in death, resurrection, and ascension.

In terms of Christ's death, the Bible emphasizes: "I have been crucified with Christ" (Gal. 2:19). It further notes that "the love of Christ controls us, having concluded this, that one died for all, therefore all died; and He died for all, so that they who live might no longer live for themselves, but for Him who died and rose again on their behalf" (2 Cor. 5:14–15 NASB). Christ was crucified and died, and mysteriously through our identification with Him, we have been crucified and died with Him.

This concept of dying with Christ is especially relevant as regards our old life of sin. The Bible asks and answers a question: "How shall we who died to sin still live in it? . . . knowing this, that our old self was crucified with Him, in order that our body of sin might be done away with, so that we would no longer be slaves to sin; for he who has died is freed from sin" (Rom. 6:2, 6–7 NASB). We have died "in Christ," and so have been freed from our old identity "in Adam." We can no longer live as we used to live.

Interestingly, the first action of baptism—being lowered into the water—vividly portrays our death with Christ. Being "in Christ," we are identified with Christ's death. But our death with Christ is only part of our new identification, just as being lowered into the water is only the first step in baptism. Baptism also involves rising out of the water, portraying our resurrection to new life: "Do you not know that all of us who have been baptized into Christ Jesus have been baptized into His death? Therefore we have been buried with Him through baptism into death, so that as Christ was raised from the dead through the glory of the Father, so we too might walk in newness of life" (Rom. 6:3–4 NASB).

Just as we are identified with Christ's death, so, too, are we identified with His resurrection. Christ was resurrected, and mysteriously through our identification with Him, we have been resurrected with Him—reminding us to dedicate everything that we are and do to God so that we live for Him: "the death that He [Christ] died, He died to sin once for all; but the life that He lives, He lives to God. Even so consider yourselves to be dead to sin, but alive to God in Christ Jesus. Therefore do not let sin reign in your mortal body so that you obey its lusts, and do not go on presenting the members of your body to sin as instruments of unrighteousness; but present yourselves to God as those alive from the dead, and your members as instruments of righteousness to God" (Rom. 6:10–13 NASB). Being "in Christ," we are identified with Christ's resurrection.

The third item of our identification with Christ is His ascension: God "raised us up with Him [Christ] and seated us with Him in the heavens, in Christ Jesus" (Eph. 2:6). Christ ascended into heaven, and mysteriously through our identification with Him, we have ascended with Him and become party to the blessings involved in that event. Some of those blessings we experience in this life: God "has blessed us with every spiritual blessing in the heavens, in Christ" (Eph. 1:3). Many other blessings await us, and we will experience them for all eternity. We ascended with Christ, Paul explains, "so that in the coming ages He might display the immeasurable riches of His grace in [His] kindness to us in Christ Jesus" (Eph. 2:7). Being "in Christ," we are identified with Christ's ascension.

Christ died. Christ rose again. Christ ascended. Whatever Christ experienced, we, too, have experienced by being "in Christ." We died. We rose again. We ascended. This means that we have made a decisive break with sin and can no longer live as we lived during our sinful existence "in Adam." Also, it means that we are to dedicate everything we are and do to God, to be used to further the cause of Jesus Christ. Furthermore, it means that we exist in the realm of God's blessings, so that now and for all eternity, God richly rewards and honors us with His approval, comfort, joy and glory.

PAUSE TIME

In your own words, what does it mean that you are no longer "in Adam" but "in Christ"? How can this new identity—being united with Christ in his death, resurrection, and ascension—help you in the following areas:
- as you face temptations?
- as you seek to be free from sinful habit patterns?
- as you earn and spend your money, choose your classes and extra-curricular activities, volunteer for various causes, think about your future, and relate to those of the opposite gender?
- as you think about your own death or that of your friends and family?

CHAPTER TEN

KEEPING ON TO THE END

She sat across the office desk from me. Like many before her— and many since—she was confused and upset by the lack of assurance that she was a Christian. Though she had prayed and asked Jesus to come into her life, though she had raised her hand to accept Jesus at summer camp, though she had gone forward at church to indicate publicly her intent to live for Christ, she lacked any firm assurance that she truly belonged to Jesus Christ.

Unlike her friends, who had profoundly emotional experiences when they embraced Christ—a sense of deep conviction of sin, a feeling that a heavy weight was being lifted away, a sense of assuring peace—she had never felt much of anything whenever she had made her many commitments to Christ.

Perhaps, she wondered, she had gone about becoming a Christian the wrong way. Perhaps, she worried, she had never genuinely trusted Christ. Perhaps, she feared, she was not a disciple of Jesus at all. These gnawing doubts conspired together to paralyze her relationship with God and her ministry to others. At times she could keep the doubts at bay by persuading herself that such doubts came from the devil and therefore were wrong. At other times, however, the doubts were so strong that she would despair of ever overcoming them.

If only she could be sure.

This is where I fit into the picture. Debi had come to me for help with the assurance of salvation. Over the course of several months, I offered her counsel from the Bible, prayed for her, challenged her thinking, pointed out Christ-like changes in her life, and expressed my assurance that she was truly a follower of Jesus—in a sense, believing it for her when she could not believe it for herself. A counselor and Debi's many friends joined me in this process.

Today, Debi is a new person. On occasion, she still wrestles with some doubt, but she knows how to face it and overcome it. She lives confidently, assured that she is a maturing disciple of Jesus Christ.

Unfortunately, such uncertainty affects the lives of far too many Christians. The lack of assurance of salvation is a pervasive problem, paralyzing many genuine Christians and rendering them ineffective in the cause of Jesus Christ. When believers lack this assurance, they become fixated on themselves: Have I truly believed? Have I adequately repented of my sins? Have I embraced Christ the right way? This obsession blocks them from giving themselves wholeheartedly to others whether in communicating the gospel to non-Christians, discipling new believers, exercising their spiritual gifts to build up the church, or other areas of ministry. It muddies their relationship with God as well, due to the nagging doubt about whether they really have a personal relationship with God. It's always back to square one—am I actually a Christian?

Fortunately, as genuine Christians, we have the privilege of knowing that we truly belong to Jesus Christ. We may possess and enjoy the assurance of salvation!

But how?

For many in my place, the starting point of their counsel for Debi would be the good fruit in her life: she reads the Bible, prays, tells others about Christ, exhibits integrity, loves God and others, is self-sacrificing, helps the poor, engages actively in church ministry, and so on. Given the fact that these realities were not true of Debi formerly, they clearly testify to the fact that Jesus Christ is in her life and is transforming it; thus, she can be sure she belongs to Him. I agree with this assessment—to a point.

Though our fruit is an important element in the assurance of salvation, it was not the element that began my conversations with Debi. In fact, I consider the witness of good fruit in our lives as a small portion of the proof of our salvation, and so it should not be the starting point for giving assurance. Indeed, without its fellow items of evidence, the good fruit in our lives constitutes little more than wishful thinking—a far cry from the solid assurance that we enjoy as authentic disciples of Jesus Christ.

But if our fruit isn't the essential evidence for our salvation, what is?

PAUSE TIME

Before you read on, what would you have shared with Debi to assure her of her salvation? Do you wrestle with a lack of such assurance? Why? What have others shared with you that has been helpful or unhelpful? If we don't find assurance in our Bible-reading and praying, being patient and kind where we formerly were angry and quick-tempered—and so forth—what other possible starting point could there be?

Let's try a different starting point to gain the assurance that we truly belong to God. Let's begin with Him instead: God—the Father, Son, and Holy Spirit.

Then we'll move on to us.

The Mighty Works of God the Father in Our Lives

My starting point with Debi was with the Father's mighty work in her life. As we have learned, before she was born—even before the universe existed, from eternity past—God had chosen Debi to become His child by faith in Jesus Christ: "Blessed be the God and Father of our Lord Jesus Christ, who has blessed us with every spiritual blessing in the heavens, in Christ; for He chose us in Him, before the foundation of the world, to be holy and blameless in His sight. In love He predestined us to be adopted through Jesus Christ for Himself, according to His favor and will, to the praise of His glorious grace that He favored us with in the Beloved" (Eph. 1:3–6). God's choice of Debi—His election of her—assures her that she belongs forever to God the Father.

But given the fact that God chose Debi, how could she ever know and be sure of His election of her? Listen again to what the apostle Paul says about believers. As he expresses his thanks to God for these Christians, he does so "knowing your election, brothers loved by God. For our gospel did not come to you in word only, but also in power, in the Holy Spirit, and with much assurance. You . . . became imitators of us and of the Lord when, in spite of severe persecution, you welcomed the message with the joy from the Holy Spirit" (1 Thess. 1:4–6).

Those who are chosen by God demonstrate their election by responding positively to the gospel—it is not just a message in words, but the truth that grips their hearts—and by living as image bearers of God—like a mirror, reflecting Him in the world in which they live. So as Debi considers the wonderful changes that have taken place in her life over time, she rightly wonders, What can account for these awesome new realities? The only explanation that is possibly true is that she was chosen by God for salvation from eternity past. The Father elected her to become his daughter! She may find assurance in that mighty work of God.

Beyond this election, the Father also has regenerated Debi, causing her to be born again. As we have seen, regeneration means that we have been rescued out of spiritual death and been given a new nature. As the apostle Peter exclaims, "Blessed be the God and Father of our Lord Jesus Christ. According to His great mercy, He has given us a new birth into a living hope through the resurrection of Jesus Christ from the dead" (1 Pet. 1:3). As Debi's new nature expresses itself—she practices righteous living, she becomes progressively free from persistent sin, she develops an authentic love for others, she increasingly resists temptations toward sin, she successfully repels the attacks of the evil one—Debi's spiritual transformation, or regeneration, emphasizes the Father's mighty work in her life and gives her assurance that she truly belongs to Him.

Furthermore, God has worked powerfully in Debi's life by justifying her. As we have discussed, justification refers to the "sweet exchange" by which our sins are imputed (or credited) to Jesus Christ and by which His righteousness is imputed to us. Thus, in justification, God declares us not guilty but righteous instead. This is a legal decision on the part of God the judge; His declaration makes it so. As Debi realizes more and more this mighty work of

God on her behalf, she will gain assurance that she truly belongs to Him.

As if all of this were not enough for us, God also adopts us as His children in His family. Adoption, as we have seen, means that we now relate intimately to God as our loving Father. Furthermore, it signifies that we belong to the family composed of all followers of Jesus Christ. As Debi relates personally to God as her Father—trusting Him, relying on Him, loving Him—and as she develops relationships with other Christians, she gains assurance that she truly belongs to God as His daughter.

Election. Regeneration. Justification. Adoption. These four mighty works of God the Father in the lives of believers constitute an unshakable foundation upon which we Christians can stake our assurance of truly belonging to God. God's eternal choice of us cannot be reneged on; God never changes His purpose to pursue us, find us, draw us, and save us. God's powerful transformation of us—delivering us from spiritual death into spiritual life—is irreversible. God's declaration that makes us not guilty but fully righteous in Jesus Christ is irrevocable. And God's inclusion of us into His family involves an adoption that is sealed forever. The progress of God's mighty work in our lives is so decisive that nothing can ever undo it or derail it or reverse it. In this reality, Debi—and you and I—can rest with great assurance of salvation.

The Purposes and Prayers of God the Son

To this solid foundation we may add the purposes and prayers of Jesus Christ. Listen to this conversation between the Son and the Father in which Jesus talks about His disciples: "Now, Father, glorify Me in Your presence with that glory I had with You before the world existed. I have revealed Your name to the men You gave Me from the world. They were Yours, You gave them to Me, and they have kept Your word" (John 17:5–6).

In some mysterious way, Jesus' disciples were given to Him by God the Father. Originally, they belonged to the Father; He then gave them to His Son. Because of this exchange, Jesus prayed to the Father for His disciples: "I pray for them. I am not praying for the world but for those You have given to Me, because they are Yours. . . . Holy Father, protect them by Your name . . . . I am not praying that You take them out of the world but that You protect them from the evil one" (John 17:9, 11, 15).

Jesus prayed for the Father's protection of His disciples. But His prayer did not end with the twelve apostles in mind. He also prayed for each and every Christian—including Debi, you, and me—who would follow those original disciples: "I pray not only for these, but also for those who believe in Me through their message. . . . Father, I desire those You have given Me to be with Me where I am. Then they will see My glory, which You have given Me because You loved Me before the world's foundation" (John 17:20, 24). The Son prayed that we Christians—we who formerly belonged to the Father and have been given by Him to the Son—would be with Him. Jesus prays that we will one day join Him in heaven.

Is there any reason to doubt that the Father hears and answers the prayers of His Son? If the answer is no—and surely, the answer is negative—then we can be confident that when we end our time on earth, we will go to be with Jesus Christ forever. Our confidence is heightened by the fact that the will of the Father is that the Son lose none of those given to Him: "Everyone the Father gives Me will come to Me, and the one who comes to Me I will never cast out. For I have come down from heaven, not to do My will, but the will of Him who sent Me. This is the will of Him who sent Me: that I should lose none of those He has given Me but should raise them up on the last day. For this is the will of My Father: that everyone who sees the Son and believes in Him may have eternal life, and I will raise him up on the last day" (John 6:37–40). As the Son always accomplished the Father's will during His earthly ministry, so we may count on Him to do so now. It is the Father's will that we who believe in Jesus Christ be raised to eternal life.

Interestingly, Jesus never ceases to pray on our behalf. As we have seen, one aspect of Jesus' current ministry in heaven is intercession or prayer for us. He constantly offers up prayers for our being with Him, for our completed salvation: "He is always able to save those who come to God through Him, since He always lives to make intercede for them" (Heb. 7:25). This verse offers great assurance: Jesus is praying for us to join Him in heaven.

Along with these prayers comes strong protection while we are living and following Christ on earth. As Jesus Himself notes: "My sheep hear My voice, I know them, and they follow Me. I give them eternal life, and they will never perish—ever! No one will snatch them out of My hand. My Father, who has given them to Me, is greater than all. No one is able to snatch them out of the Father's hand. The Father and I are one" (John 10:27–30).

Actually, there is a dual protection plan in place for us as disciples of Jesus: Both He—the good shepherd, who cares for and protects His sheep—and the Father hold us in their mighty hands. No one—deceivers, enemies, persecutors, false leaders—and no thing—demonic forces, temptation, sin, death—can ever break the grip of the Father and the Son and successfully snatch us out of their protective care. So the mission of the Son—to give eternal life to all those given to Him by the Father, including Debi, you, and me—can never be frustrated. In this, we may find great assurance.

The Power of God the Holy Spirit

The third aspect of our foundation for assurance of salvation involves the Holy Spirit. With respect to Him, we must consider His sealing ministry or pledge of salvation, His internal witness to the fact that we truly belong to God, and His powerful transforming work in our life.

When we became Christians, something mysterious happened to us: "In Him [Christ], you also, after listening to the message of truth, the gospel of your salvation—having also believed, you were sealed in Him with the Holy Spirit of promise, who is given as a pledge of our inheritance, with a view to the redemption of God's own possession, to the praise of His glory" (Eph. 1:13–14 NASB). The Holy Spirit sealed us when we became followers of Jesus Christ, indelibly marking us as belonging to God. So we bear a seal testifying to the fact that we are Christians.

The Spirit also is described as a pledge of our inheritance or a down payment. We recently went house-hunting in Louisville, Kentucky, where we now live. When we discovered a house that seemed to be good to buy, we put down $2,000 as "earnest money" to express our serious intention to purchase the home for the full price of $200,000. This down payment indicated to the sellers that within two months, we would have the rest of the money to complete the purchase.

In a similar way, the Holy Spirit is a down payment of our salvation. He is a type of divine promise, indicating that what God has initiated in our life now will be completed when we go to be with Jesus. In other words, what we have received from God in this lifetime is only a portion of what is yet to come. We have God's blessings—but only in part. We have experienced salvation—but only in part. We have a relationship with God—but only in part. In one sense, the best is yet to come! And the Holy Spirit is God's guarantee that we will one day receive all that we now can only anticipate. Again, this gives us great assurance that we belong to God.

In addition to sealing us, the Holy Spirit also testifies that we belong to God: "The Spirit Himself testifies together with our spirit that we are God's children" (Rom. 8:16). This internal witness of the Holy Spirit is rather difficult to explain, but involves the firm conviction that we sense in our hearts as believers that we are truly saved and belong to God forever.

Just seconds after I committed my life to Jesus Christ as a senior in high school, I had this overwhelming sense that I now possessed eternal life. At the time, I had no idea where that notion came from; it was not as if someone told me about it. Only later, when I read Romans 8:16, did I come to realize that the Holy Spirit was giving me internal assurance that I had become a child of God. This assurance is the privilege of every believer in Jesus Christ. The Spirit's testimony in your life may be different from His witness in my life, but you still can hear His assuring work and gain confidence that you are truly a follower of Christ.

In addition to His pledge and internal witness, the Holy Spirit also works powerfully to change our lives to better reflect the image of Christ. The apostle Paul underscores this reality: "Now the Lord is the Spirit, and where the Spirit of the Lord is, there is liberty. But we all, with unveiled face, beholding as in a mirror the glory of the Lord, are being transformed into the same image from glory to glory, just as from the Lord, the Spirit" (2 Cor. 3:17–18 NASB).

The Holy Spirit is powerfully at work to transform us from cracked and broken mirrors—the image bearers of God ruined by sin and evil—into ones that progressively and more authentically reflect the character of God. Created for the purpose of imaging God, we miserably failed in this calling before we embraced Jesus Christ. Now as His followers, we are enabled by the powerful transformative power of the Holy Spirit to be what God intended us to be: restored mirrors that genuinely reflect Him to our families, friends, fellow students in school, colleagues at work, and other Christians at church. As we reflect the character of Christ, we can gain great assurance that we belong to God because we experience the power of the Holy Spirit in our lives.

The Promises of God's Word

To this triune work of God the Father, God the Son, and God the Holy Spirit, we may add another strong foundational aspect for our assurance of salvation. This aspect involves the many promises of eternal life given to us in the Word of God.

In a very straightforward statement, the apostle John notes: "And this is the testimony: God has given us eternal life, and this life is in His Son. The one who has the Son has life. The one who doesn't have the Son of God does not have life. I have written these things to you who believe in the name of the Son of God, so that you may know that you have eternal life" (1 John 5:11–13).

God's gift of eternal life is tied up with Jesus Christ. Whoever has Jesus has this life, an eternal relationship with God. Whoever does not have Jesus is missing this life. This promise is given to us disciples of Jesus, not that we may merely wish, hope, dream, or imagine that we might possibly have this life, but that we may know—confidently, definitely, assuredly—that we have eternal life. What is required on our part is trust in this divine promise. Of course, we may choose not to believe what God has said. The result of this, however, will be constant doubts about our salvation. But knowing that God always speaks the truth and is always faithful to fulfill His promises, we may unwaveringly count on God to give us eternal life as He has promised.

PAUSE TIME

Trust God's promises about His work in your life.

- "For I am confident of this very thing, that He who began a good work in you will perfect it until the day of Christ Jesus" (Phil. 1:6 NASB). As God has initiated His work of salvation in your life, can you confidently trust that He will continue working in your life to free you from sin, transform you into the image of Christ, deliver you from temptation, protect you from the evil one, and develop love for Him and others?
- "I know whom I have believed and I am convinced that He is able to guard what I have entrusted to Him until that day" (2 Tim. 1:12 NASB). Can you confidently trust that God is able to protect what you have staked your life upon?
- "For I am convinced that neither death, nor life, nor angels, nor principalities, nor things present, nor things to come, nor powers, nor height, nor depth, nor any other created thing, will be able to separate us from the love of God, which is in Christ Jesus our Lord" (Rom. 8:38-39 NASB). Can you confidently trust that there is not one person, not one spiritual creature (either demonic or angelic), not any reality nor any unreality that exists now or forevermore that is able to keep you from enjoying God's blessings of salvation?

Trust in the promises of the Word of God gives us great assurance of salvation.

Good Fruit in Our Lives

At the beginning of our discussion on the assurance of salvation (and Debi's struggles with it), I noted that for many people in my place of advising her, the starting point for their counsel would be the good fruit in her life. As you can see, the fruit is the fifth and final aspect that I shared with Debi. As important and necessary as this good fruit is—reading the Bible, praying, telling others about Christ, exhibiting integrity, loving God and others, being self-sacrificing, helping the poor, engaging actively in church ministry, and so on—it is not the point with which I started.

Why not?

Again, let me underscore something: evidence of a transformed life is absolutely crucial for us as followers of Jesus Christ. Conversion—repentance from sin and faith in Jesus Christ—will always produce new realities that were not true of us formerly. As such, they clearly testify to the fact that Jesus Christ is in our lives; these new realities are evidence that we truly belong to Him and give us assurance. In the words of 1 John 2:3-6: "By this we know that we have come to know Him, if we keep His commandments. The one who says, 'I have come to know Him,' and does not keep His commandments, is a liar, and the truth is not in him; but whoever keeps His word, in him the love of God has truly been perfected. By this we know that we are in Him: the one who says he abides in Him ought himself to walk in the same manner as He walked" (NASB). We as true disciples reflect the image of our Lord and Savior Jesus Christ. Our life bears witness that we truly belong to Him.

Despite this witness, I don't begin with this evidence of a transformed life when giving assurance of salvation. One reason for this is the good fruit in our life is sometimes difficult to assess because it is subjectively evaluated. For example, Debi was confused by comparing what happened to her after numerous times of accepting Jesus into her life with what happened to her friends when they embraced Christ. They had profound emotional experiences—they felt the weight of sin lifting off their shoulders, they cried, they sensed deep peace. Debi did not. Something else happened to her, but it was difficult to assess because it was not as evident as what had happened to her friends. So right away, Debi became frustrated with the good fruit in her life. Her conversion didn't match up with that of her friends—that is, it wasn't as sensational—so she concluded something was wrong with her. She must not be truly saved.

Debi's problem arose from comparing herself with her friends. Another problem can arise when we compare our actions and thoughts with our own high expectations. Many of us have an idea of what we should be like as Christians: we always overcome temptation, we regularly lead people to Christ, we pray often and God answers our prayers miraculously, and so forth. This is a "phantom" notion of what we should be like as followers of Jesus—a lofty, but unattainable ideal. But we hold ourselves to this phantom ideal and inevitably fall short. If we do this enough times, we soon become discouraged and depressed and wonder how we could be such miserable Christians—if we are Christians at all! Once again, the misguided perspective on the fruit in our lives dashes our assurance to pieces.

But there is another important reason to refrain from initially focusing on the good fruit in our lives in discussing assurance of salvation. Good fruit—character change, new purpose in life, power for ministry—is just that: fruit. And fruit is a product that is produced by someone or something *other than us*. As Jesus explains, "I am the vine; you are the branches. The one who remains in Me and I in him produces much fruit, because you can do nothing without Me" (John 15:5).

Good fruit points to something beyond itself. For this reason, I don't begin with the fruit itself but with its source: the works of God the Father, God the Son, and God the Holy Spirit. Our assurance must be grounded on those realities, and those realities—election, justification, regeneration, adoption, intercession, protection, sealing, internal witness, transformation—are the source of the good fruit anyway. As we see our lives changed and good fruit produced, our assurance does not rest on that evidence but on the realities that bring forth the changed life and good fruit.

Here's a graphic representation of the magnitude of these realities:

Good Fruit in Our Life
The Promises of God's Word
The Power of God the Holy Spirit
The Purposes and Prayers of God the Son
The Mighty Works of God the Father in Our Lives

Notice the solid foundation: the Father's mighty works, the Son's purposes and prayers, and the Spirit's power. To this is added the promises of God's Word. On top of this foundation—and clearly resting upon it—is the good fruit in our life. What would happen if the triangle were reversed? It would become quite unstable. So don't begin with the good fruit. Make sure the evidence of a changed life is supported by the solid foundation of the work of the triune God. From this we may draw strong assurance of our salvation.

PAUSE TIME

How are you doing with the assurance of your salvation? Do you
have doubts that you truly belong to Jesus? Are these doubts
persistent or only occasional? Are you paralyzed with fear of
not being a follower of Christ? Have you become fixated on yourself, asking over and over again: Have I truly believed? Have
I adequately repented of my sins? Have I embraced Christ the
right way?

Many Christians lack confidence in this area. This may be
due to persistent sin. One area or several areas of habitual
sin constantly defeat Christians' intentions to be good followers of Christ, so they lose confidence. Demonic deception may
be involved as well. As one theologian noted: "Satan has no
more grievous or dangerous temptation to dishearten believers
than when he unsettles them with doubt about their election."[19]
Others are depressed or full of personal anxiety, which clouds
their ability to be sure. Some find themselves unable to trust
the biblical promises of assurance. In many cases, Christians
are simply ignorant of the scriptural teaching on assurance.

Are any of these scenarios true of you? What aspects of
our discussion could be helpful in firming up your sense of assurance? Also, do you know Christians who are wrestling with
this issue? What could you share to help give them assurance of
salvation?

One more reality remains for us to discuss: All of us know people who have professed to be Christians but then have fallen away
from Christ, abandoned God, and turned their life in the wrong
direction. Perhaps some of these have been close friends of ours, so
we feel particularly confused about and concerned for them. Did
these people lose their salvation? Were they even disciples of Jesus
in the first place? If so, how could it be that they were so committed to Christ and active in ministry, but now are so far from the
Lord?

Also, we may be familiar with the expression "once saved,
always saved," meaning that once we have embraced Christ, we
cannot lose our salvation. So if these people who have fallen away
from Christ were once saved, then they cannot lose their salvation.
Or can they?

Follow me on this one: First, what I have said about the assurance of salvation does not apply to everyone who professes to
be a Christian, but only to those who truly belong to Christ. Only

if we are genuine followers of Jesus can we enjoy the assurance of belonging to Him forever. Many people profess to be Christians yet lack the assurance of salvation. That is as it should be because they are not true disciples of Jesus Christ.

Second, it sometimes is very difficult to know if some people are genuine believers; some nonbelievers profess to be Christians and even give startling evidence of conversion to Christ. But listen to what Jesus says: "Not everyone who says to Me, 'Lord, Lord!' will enter the kingdom of heaven, but [only] the one who does the will of My Father in heaven. On that day many will say to Me, 'Lord, Lord, didn't we prophesy in Your name, drive out demons in Your name, and do many miracles in Your name?' Then I will announce to them, 'I never knew you! Depart from Me, you lawbreakers!'" (Matt. 7:21–23).

Imagine the surprise of these people as they face Jesus on the day of judgment. They received and communicated revelations from God, they cast out demons, and they performed miracles—all in the name of Jesus! But they never truly belonged to Him. Certainly, they gave startling evidence of being His followers, yet they were not genuine disciples of Christ.

Or consider this description of certain people in the early church:

> For in the case of those who have once been enlightened and have tasted of the heavenly gift and have been made partakers of the Holy Spirit, and have tasted the good word of God and the powers of the age to come, and then have fallen away, it is impossible to renew them again to repentance, since they again crucify to themselves the Son of God and put Him to open shame. For ground that drinks the rain which often falls on it and brings forth vegetation useful to those for whose sake it is also tilled, receives a blessing from God; but if it yields thorns and thistles, it is worthless and close to being cursed, and it ends up being burned. (Heb. 6:4–8 NASB)

At first reading, we automatically assume that this description applies to people who are genuine followers of Jesus Christ. They have received answers to their prayers, the Holy Spirit has worked powerfully in and through them, they have benefited from many blessings of God, they have known the truth of the gospel, and so forth. Surely these people were true Christians! Yet, they have then fallen away—so much so, that they can never come back to the point of turning away from their sin of desertion so as to embrace Christ again.

On closer inspection, however, we understand that these people never were disciples of Jesus in the first place. Notice the description of the well-watered soil: if it yields good fruit (as a genuine Christian would), it receives God's blessing (as a genuine Christian would). But if it produces weeds (as a nonbeliever would), it burns in the end (as a nonbeliever would). Now the people described in this passage did not receive a blessing from God; thus, they were not genuine disciples. Rather, they fall away and burn in the end; thus, they were nonbelievers.

So as to confirm this understanding, the passage continues: "But, beloved, we are convinced of better things concerning you, and things that accompany salvation, though we are speaking in this way. For God is not unjust so as to forget your work and the love which you have shown toward His name, in having ministered and in still ministering to the saints" (Heb. 6:9–10 NASB). What could possibly be better than being the type of people described in the first part of the passage? Being true followers of Jesus Christ, having experienced genuine conversion, and engaging in good works of love toward God and others. And the writer of this passage says this is true of his readers—they are genuine Christians. But certainly his description helps us to realize that some people in our own church—those who sit in the pews or chairs next to us, our worship leaders, Sunday school teachers, even our pastors and ministers—may profess to be Christians, may give startling evidence of being saved, yet may not be authentic disciples of Jesus Christ.

PAUSE TIME

What do you make of this? Does this frighten you? If our Sunday school teachers and senior pastors could end up not being true Christians, what does that mean for us? If the best examples of Christians that we know may not be genuine, what about those of us who struggle and barely make it?

Let me assure you: God never intended this passage to dis-
turb and upset you about the genuineness of your faith in Jesus
Christ. If you are a true disciple—trusting God more and more,
obeying Christ more and more, yielding to the Spirit's direction
more and more—then why would God want to cause you worry or
place doubts in your mind about being His child?

I have never once said to my three loving and obedient children, "But if you ever turn bad, I will disown you!"
How cruel would that be! And if that is unworthy of any good
earthly father (or mother), how much more is it unworthy of
God our heavenly Father? God did not intend for this passage to
alarm you. He actually is saying this to people who are consid-
ering leaving the faith and abandoning Jesus Christ. To them—
not to genuine believers—God offers a frightening warning: If
you ever go down that path and fall away, there is absolutely
no hope for you whatsoever. Don't do it!

So don't embark on a secret spy mission to identify false
disciples and weed them out from the true disciples. They will
do that themselves, as another passages tell us: "They went
out from us, but they were not really of us; for if they had
been of us, they would have remained with us; but they went
out, so that it would be shown that they all are not of us"
(1 John 2:19). As you see, true believers remain in community
with other true believers. They continue to be involved in
church because they are genuine disciples. Those who only profess faith in Christ but do not truly belong to Him leave the
community of faith. They abandon the church, because they are
not genuine disciples.

So be aware of those who leave your church. If they fall
away, they were not authentic followers of Christ in the first
place. But don't be worried about the genuineness of your own
faith. Continue to trust and obey Jesus, and you will have
great assurance of belonging to Him.

And now to my third point: When these nonbelievers (who
give startling evidence of belonging to Christ) turn away, they fall
away not from true faith in Jesus but from a religious position
they once held. They were never genuine believers in the first place,
so they don't lose their salvation. Rather, they turn away from a
religious commitment—being involved in church, helping others,
working for Christ, agreeing that Christianity is a good religion
and lifestyle—which is very, very different from a personal relationship with God.

Because it is with God that we enjoy this relationship that lasts
forever, we can look to Him to preserve us throughout our walk

of faith in this life and lead us all the way to its end. As the Bible underscores, we are given "an inheritance that is imperishable, uncorrupted, and unfading, kept in heaven for you, who are being protected by God's power through faith for a salvation that is ready to be revealed in the last time" (1 Pet. 1:4–5). This perseverance is God's work in our life: He Himself guards us and keeps us safe from any and all obstacles—fierce temptations, demonic attacks, trials that loom large, discouragement—that attempt to distract and detour us. That is God's work of preservation.

But we have our own responsibility in this as well: we must continue in faith, trusting God each and every moment of our life. That faith is built by study of His Word, by praying, by being in community with other believers, and so forth. So God is engaged in protecting us, and we are engaged in trusting Him. As He preserves us through our persevering faith, we can gain great confidence that we are genuine disciples of Jesus.

PAUSE TIME

The history of the church is filled with outstanding examples of men and women who, possessing a deep sense of assurance of salvation, faced incredible odds—persecution, confiscation of property, imprisonment, even death—and spread the good news of Jesus Christ around the world. You see, if your eternal destiny is assured—if you know you will be with Christ forever when you die—then what could grip your heart with ultimate fear? What could cause you to pull back with concern? What could detour you from risking everything for the cause of Christ? If nothing can stop you—even martyrdom means entering immediately into Christ's presence—what is holding you back from making whatever commitment Jesus is asking you to make?

Don't hesitate. Don't wait. If Jesus is calling you to commit to Him, then do it now—and don't ever look back.

"BUT YOU—WHO DO YOU SAY THAT I AM?"

This book began by noting an incident in the life of Jesus (Matt. 16:13–16). In a conversation with His disciples, He first asked them, "Who do people say that the Son of Man is?" After hearing some of the popular opinions about His identity, Jesus directed a second—and personal—question to His disciples: "But you—who do you say that I am?" Peter's response, which was revealed to him by God the Father, was right on target: "You are the Messiah, the Son of the living God!"

As it did nearly two thousand years ago, the same question resounds today from the lips of Jesus Christ to His current disciples. Specifically, it is a question that Jesus personally directs to you. The question is a weighty one—the most important question in the universe! Your answer to it will determine your destiny—both in this life and for all eternity.

This book has looked at what the Bible affirms about Jesus Christ in order to help you answer this question in an accurate, personally satisfying way. Jesus is fully God—exactly like the Father in every way. Jesus is fully man—exactly like you and me in every way, except He is without sin. Jesus is Immanuel, God-with-us, God in the flesh, the God-man. WDJD? Jesus engaged in teaching, discipling, facing conflicts, furthering the kingdom of God, and relating to both the Father and the Holy Spirit. Furthermore, Jesus died and was buried. On the third day, Jesus rose from the dead. Forty days later, Jesus ascended into heaven.

We then dove into the application of Jesus' atoning work on the cross and His resurrection to our life. From eternity past, God chose us to experience salvation (election). In time, when we heard the gospel, we chose God through repentance from sin and faith in Jesus Christ (conversion). Furthermore, God acts powerfully to accomplish an awesome, multi-faceted work in our lives: we are born again (regeneration), we are declared not guilty but righteous instead (justification), we join a new family (adoption), and we gain a new identity (we are "in Christ"). And God's work will continue throughout our lives. Indeed, by His powerful persevering work we are protected through our faith, so that we will remain Christians until the very end of our lives. This reality provides us with the assurance of salvation.

So what is your answer to Jesus' question: "But you—who do you say that I am?" Remember, any proper answer encompasses far more than mere intellectual assent to the person and work of Christ. Your answer must go beyond checking off ideas in your mind:

✓ Jesus is fully God.
✓ Jesus is fully man.
✓ Jesus is the Savior who died for my sins.

Though each of these is true, intellectual assent to them is not an adequate response. Listen to how Jesus Himself defined eternal life—the gift we receive from God when we embrace His Son—in a prayer to the Father: "This is eternal life: that they may know You, the only true God, and the One You have sent—Jesus Christ" (John 17:3). More than just a cognitive response, your answer to Jesus' question involves a personal, intimate relationship with the Father and with Him. It involves love, enduring commitment, thankfulness, obedience, trust, submission, joy, faithfulness, testing, contentment, sacrifice, comfort, suffering, and much more.

Perhaps more than anything else, a proper response to Jesus' question commits you to worshipping Him. This is the response we see time and again by those who embrace Jesus. The first act performed by the wise men when they arrived in Bethlehem, having followed the star from their eastern lands to find the one "who has been born King of the Jews" (Matt. 2:2), was to worship Jesus: "Entering the house, they saw the child with Mary His mother, and falling to their knees, they worshipped Him. Then they opened their treasures and presented Him with gifts: gold, frankincense, and myrrh" (Matt. 2:11).

During Jesus' ministry, worship was the response of people to His miraculous healing. The disciples, for example, saw Jesus walking on the water while a strong wind was blowing and the waters were rough (they were straining against the oars). At first, they mistook Him for a ghost. Though Jesus assured them otherwise, Peter insisted that, if it were indeed Jesus who was approaching their boat, Jesus should command him to come closer by walking on the water. Though he started out well, Peter was quickly seized by fear of the gale-like winds and began to sink. "Immediately Jesus reached out His hand, caught hold of him, and said to him, 'You of little faith, why did you doubt?' When they got into the boat, the wind ceased. Then those in the boat worshipped Him and said, 'Truly You are the Son of God!'" (Matt. 14:31–33).

Worship was also the response of the man who was born blind but was healed by Jesus. Because the miracle was not instantaneous (Jesus made some mud from His own saliva and dirt from the ground, then applied that compound to the man's eyes and ordered him to wash in a pool; John 9:6–7), the healed man had never seen Jesus. Jesus "found him and asked, 'Do you believe in the Son of Man?' 'Who is He, Sir, that I may believe in Him?' he asked. Jesus answered, 'You have seen Him; in fact, He is the One speaking with you.' 'I believe, Lord!' he said, and he worshipped Him" (John 9:35–38).

Like the wise men, the disciples, the man born blind, and countless others, will you respond to the question posed to you by Jesus—"But you—who do you say that I am?"—not only with the proper answer, but also with worship?

PAUSE TIME

Here's my final challenge: As you respond to the question Jesus asks you—"But you—who do you say that I am?"— think how the relationship offered by a proper and personally satisfying answer includes the following elements:

- Love: "'Love the Lord your God with all your heart, with all your soul, and with all your mind.' This is

the greatest and most important commandment. The
second is like it: 'Love your neighbor as yourself'"
(Matt. 22:37-39).

* Enduring commitment: "May you be strengthened with all
  power, according to His glorious might, for all endur-
  ance and patience" (Col. 1:11).
* Thankfulness: "Giving thanks always for everything to
  God the Father in the name of our Lord Jesus Christ"
  (Eph. 5:20).
* Obedience: "We demolish arguments and every high-
  minded thing that is raised up against the knowledge of
  God, taking every thought captive to the obedience of
  Christ" (2 Cor. 10:4-5).
* Hope: "We also groan within ourselves, eagerly waiting
  for adoption, the redemption of our bodies. Now in this
  hope we were saved, yet hope that is seen is not hope,
  because who hopes for what he sees? But if we hope for
  what we do not see, we eagerly wait for it with patience" (Rom. 8:23-25).
* Joy: "You love Him, though you have not seen Him. And
  though not seeing Him now, you believe in Him and rejoice with inexpressible and glorious joy, because you
  are receiving the goal of your faith, the salvation of
  your souls" (1 Pet. 1:8-9).
* Faithfulness: "But now He has reconciled you by His
  physical body through His death, to present you holy,
  faultless, and blameless before Him—if indeed you remain grounded and steadfast in the faith, and are not
  shifted away from the hope of the gospel you heard"
  (Col. 1:22-23).
* Testing: "You rejoice in this, though now for a short
  time you have had to be distressed by various trials so
  that the genuineness of your faith—more valuable than
  gold, which perishes though refined by fire—may result
  in praise, glory, and honor at the revelation of Jesus
  Christ" (1 Pet. 1:6-7).
* Contentment: "I have learned to be content in whatever circumstances I am. I know both how to have a
  little, and I know how to have a lot. In any and all
  circumstances I have learned the secret [of being con-
  tent]—whether well-fed or hungry, whether in abundance
  or in need. I am able to do all things through Him who
  strengthens me" (Phil. 4:11-13).
* Sacrifice: "But everything that was a gain to me, I have
  considered to be a loss because of Christ. More than
  that, I also consider everything to be a loss in view of
  the surpassing value of knowing Christ Jesus my Lord"
  (Phil. 3:7-8).

- Suffering: "For it has been given to you on Christ's behalf not only to believe in Him, but also to suffer for Him" (Phil. 1:29).
- Comfort: God "comforts us in all our affliction, so that we may be able to comfort those who are in any kind of affliction, through the comfort we ourselves receive from God. For as the sufferings of Christ overflow to us, so our comfort overflows through Christ" (2 Cor. 1:4-5).
- Worship:
    They said with a loud voice:
        The Lamb who was slaughtered is worthy
        to receive power and riches
        and wisdom and strength
        and honor and glory and blessing!
    I heard every creature in heaven, on earth,
    under the earth, on the sea, and everything
    in them say:
        Blessing and honor and glory and dominion
        to the One seated on the throne,
        and to the Lamb, forever and ever!
    (Rev. 5:12-13).

So respond rightly to Jesus' question. Intimately relate to Him. Worship Him faithfully and passionately—not only because He is the only one worthy of our honor and praise, but also because worshipping Jesus the Lamb of God is your destiny for all eternity.

CREDITS

Many people and resources have contributed to the development of my theology, but none more than my good friend Wayne Grudem. Much of the material in chapters 2, 3, 4, 8, 9, and 10 reflects this influence and its expression in his book *Systematic Theology: An Introduction to Biblical Doctrine* (Leicester, England: InterVarsity and Grand Rapids: Zondervan, 1994).

NOTES

1. The Council of Nicea met in AD 325. The *Creed of Nicea,* which was produced by the council, affirmed the identity of Jesus Christ as fully God and condemned all the false beliefs of Arius. Though it would be about fifty years before all the churches accepted the *Creed of Nicea* as the official statement of faith of the church, it has never wavered from affirming the deity of Jesus Christ.

2. *Apostles' Creed.*

3. B. B. Warfield, *The Person and Work of Christ* (Philadelphia: Presbyterian and Reformed, 1970), 116–17.

4. Historically, this has been referred to as Apollinarianism.

5. Historically, this view has been held by Protestant liberals.

6. John Hick, *The Myth of God Incarnate* (Louisville: Westminster John Knox, 1977), 11.

7. Melito of Sardis, *The Discourse on the Cross,* in Alexander Roberts and James Donaldson, eds., *Ante-Nicene Fathers* (Edinburgh: T & T Clark and Grand Rapids: Eerdmans), 8:756.

8. Wayne Grudem, *Systematic Theology: An Introduction to Biblical Doctrine* (Leicester, England: InterVarsity and Grand Rapids: Zondervan, 1994), 543.

9. *Creed of Chalcedon* in Philip Schaff, *Creeds of Christendom,* vol. 2: *The Greek and Latin Creeds* (Grand Rapids: Baker, 1931), 62–63.

10. Historically, this has been referred to as Nestorianism.

11. Historically, this has been referred to as Eutychianism.

12. *Athanasian Creed* in Schaff, *Creeds of Christendom,* 68–69.

13. If you are familiar with C. S. Lewis's *The Chronicles of Narnia,* you should recall Aslan the lion (who is a symbol of Jesus Christ), who is described as "not a tame lion" throughout the series. More specifically, the Mr. Beaver character says that Aslan "Isn't safe. But

he's good, He's the King," in *The Lion, the Witch, and the Wardrobe* (New York: HarperTrophy, 1994), 80.

14. A helpful definition, though somewhat technical, of a parable is the following: "It expresses or implies the logic of analogy in the language of either simile or metaphor elaborated into a form of allegory that is selectively, but not pervasively, symbolic." John W. Sider, *Interpreting the Parables* (Grand Rapids: Zondervan, 1995), 259.

15. The order of the temptations is different in Matthew and Luke, and I have followed that of Matthew. He gives a chronological order, as indicated by his attention to temporal sequence ("then"; Matt. 4:1, 5, 11), whereas Luke inverts the second and third temptations for his own purposes.

16. Francis A. Schaeffer, *The Mark of the Christian* (Downers Grove: InterVarsity, 1970).

17. Second Timothy 1:9 adds that God "has saved us, and called us with a holy calling, not according to our works, but according to His own purpose and grace which was given to us in Christ Jesus before time began."

18. Most likely, Jesus was referring to a prophecy that had been given to God's people centuries prior to His earthly ministry: "Then I will sprinkle clean water on you, and you will be clean; I will cleanse you from all your filthiness and from all your idols. Moreover, I will give you a new heart and put a new spirit within you; and I will remove the heart of stone from your flesh and give you a heart of flesh. And I will put My Spirit within you and cause you to walk in My statutes, and you will be careful to observe all My ordinances" (Ezek. 36:25–27). That is why, later in His conversation with Nicodemus, Jesus could express surprise that His friend, as "the teacher of Israel," did not understand His words about the new birth (John 3:10). Nicodemus should have been familiar with Ezekiel's prophecy and related it to what Jesus was saying about being born again of water and the Spirit, two key images in that prophecy.

19. John Calvin, *Institutes of the Christian Religion* 3.24.4, in *The Library of Christian Classics*, vol. 21 (Philadelphia: Westminster, 1960), 968.

Don't miss these other great resources for students.